Trans-Lated

Translation and Cultural Manipulation

Said Faiq

UNIVERSITY PRESS OF AMERICA,® INC.
Lanham • Boulder • New York • Toronto • Plymouth, UK

Copyright © 2007 by
University Press of America,® Inc.
4501 Forbes Boulevard
Suite 200
Lanham, Maryland 20706
UPA Acquisitions Department (301) 459-3366

Estover Road
Plymouth PL6 7PY
United Kingdom

Library of Congress Control Number: 2007923880
ISBN-13: 978-0-7618-3748-0 (paperback : alk. paper)
ISBN-10: 0-7618-3748-5 (paperback : alk. paper)

$\bigotimes^{TM}$ The paper used in this publication meets the minimum
requirements of American National Standard for Information
Sciences—Permanence of Paper for Printed Library Materials,
ANSI Z39.48—1984

To Payman, Elyas, and Lanya.

Contents

Preface

Literature is not innocent. Neither is translation.

(Carol Coates 1996, 215)

In July 2006 at the G8 summit in Russia, unknown to him that the microphone was still on when he was discussing the armed conflict between Lebanon's Hizbollah and Israel with the British Prime Minister, Tony Blair, the United States President, George W. Bush, used the four-letter word 'shit' to describe the conflict; a conflict that killed hundreds of innocent civilians and forced thousands of Lebanon-loving Westerners to flee the country.

Mr. Bush's choice of word fits his overall culture and its associated master discourse of representation. What is at stake here is that non-Western cultures and societies have been represented and translated according to fixed ideologies and discursive strategies. Africans, Arabs, Muslims and Israelis, as well as Central and Eastern Europeans are all still seen as trouble-makers and sources of nuisance for the Western world, which finds itself time and again having to intervene to solve their problems and bickering.

Regarding the choice of terms to describe other cultures and/or concepts in these cultures, Jim Garamone (2006) of the American Forces Press Service, reporting on a study by Dr. Douglas E. Streusand and Army Lt. Col. Harry D. Tunnell IV of the National Defense University at Fort Lesley J. McNair in Washington, D.C., noted that 'in the war of words we [USA] unwittingly give the advantage to the enemy.' Particularly when dealing with cultures like Islam,

American leaders misuse language to such a degree that they unintentionally wind up promoting the ideology of the groups the United States is fighting . . . A case in point is the term "jihadist." Many leaders use the term jihadist or jihadi as a synonym for Islamic extremist. Jihad has been commonly adapted in

English as meaning "holy war." But to Muslims it means much more . . . [Jihad] literally means striving and generally occurs as part of the expression 'jihad fi sabil illah,' striving in the path of God . . . Calling our enemies jihadis and their movement a global jihad thus indicates that we recognize their doctrines and actions as being in the path of God and, for Muslims, legitimate. By countering jihadis, the West and moderate Muslims are enemies of true Islam.

Within intercultural encounters and particularly in a colonial and post-colonial context, translation, as Niranjana (1992, 1) succinctly writes

becomes a significant site for raising questions of representation, power, and historicity. The context is one of contested stories attempting to account for, to recount, the asymmetry and inequality of relations between peoples, races, languages.

The examination of the links between translation from, including writings about, non-dominant cultures into dominant and hegemonic ones is not entirely new. Referring to translation into German, Rudolf Pannwitz (cited in Dingwaney 1995, 7) pointed out the basic flaws of translation and translators:

Our translations, even the best ones, proceed from the wrong premise. They want to turn Hindi, Greek, English, into German, instead of turning German into Hindi, Greek, or English. Our translators have a far greater reverence for their language than for the spirit of the foreign languages . . . The basic error of the translator is that he preserves the state in which his own language happens to be instead of allowing his language to be powerfully affected by the foreign tongue.

Though contemporary translation studies has managed to rid itself, albeit not entirely, of the notions of equivalence, accuracy, fidelity, free vs. literal methods, its emerging sites of intercultural communication are bound, however, to make it the site for the contestation of the spaces between cultures and relationships of power and knowledge. These relationships are precisely the prime movers behind this book. Its hyphenated title *trans-lated* is intended to show the manipulation inherent in translation and the fractures it causes.

So, within the cultural circuit of translation studies, this book addresses questions of meaning, language, identity, and representation: images and concepts that trigger smooth or conflictual outcome of intercultural communication whether through translation proper (chapters 1, 2 and 5), self-translation (chapter 4), or pseudo-translation (chapter 3).

Chapter 1 sets the scene and tone of the volume. It outlines the relationship between culture and translation concluding that the translation of culture is intrinsically bound up with the culture of translation.

Continuing the arguments of chapter 1, chapter 2 discusses the existence of a master discourse that underlines and animates translation projects and practices. Drawing on translation from Arabic and the representations of this language and its associated culture in and by Western languages and cultures, the chapter discusses how exotic, manipulating, subverting and appropriating translation strategies still govern intercultural encounters through translation from Arabic and associated representations of its speakers.

The hybrid nature of the relationship between the ex-colonizer's epistemology and the desire to (re)create an independent identity within post-colonial cultures is the theme of chapter 3, which presents a reading of Arabic literature written in French by Arabs but within the requirements of the master discourse of the French culture. It also examines how translations of such literature back into Arabic represent no more than pseudo-translations (not true or real). The accepted body of this literature in the French literary and cultural arenas represents a cultural dislocation caused by 'native foreigners,' who adhere to the politics of exotica, violence, greed and barbarism that are the main pillars of the master discourse of translation from and representation of the Arabs and Islam within mainstream French culture.

Following on from chapter 3, chapter 4 raises the issue of self-translation and associated questions of identity and power. The chapter considers two instances of self-translation: an Arab author writing in English and deciding to translate his text into Arabic for his fellow Arabs with all the manipulatory strategies he allows himself, and a culture deciding to self-translate perhaps to protect its culture and master discourse from manipulation, invisibility, domestication, and subversion: an instance of cultural protectionism through a foreignizing translation strategy.

The final chapter discusses the question of translation historiography and its role in looking at translation projects as indices of cultural development or the lack of it. In this way, the chapter brings the discussion started in chapter 1 to a close: the translation of culture should be sought in the culture of translation.

Acknowledgments

It is not easy to actually thank all those who helped in many ways in the evolution of the ideas and arguments expounded in this modest volume. Still, I am most grateful to the hundreds of undergraduate and graduate students at Salford and Leeds Universities, UK, and at the American University of Sharjah, United Arab Emirates, for their lively debates and discussions about the points and views outlined here.

I am also thankful to the many reviewers and editors and colleagues who, over the past decade, commented on my research and publications about the issues that animate the discussion of the present volume.

I am grateful to the technical and editorial teams at University Press of America for their support and most valuable advice.

Chapter One

The Culture of Translation and the Translation of Culture

The activity of translation has generally been practised on the basis that knowing the source and target languages represents a sufficient premise for rendering, transferring or translating texts across languages and cultures. Translators have been expected to achieve the same informational and emotive effects in their translations as those achieved by the author of the source text.

At first sight, this goal for translation might appear reasonable and achievable. Yet its implementation often, if not always, creates problems of one kind or another at one level or another or at many levels simultaneously during the translation process.

To achieve this objective, translators and translation theorists have stressed one method or another in translation and in the process they have sacrificed certain aspects of the source or target text either on the content level or the expressive (form) level depending on the guiding principles espoused. The main guiding principle, which has long loomed over the theory and practice of translation, is the notion of *equivalence*. The search for equivalence in translation has often led theorists and translators alike to focus on aspects of either the form or content, ignoring along the way the fact that any text produced in a given language is the product of a unique union between both form and content (manner and matter), and, more importantly, that it is embedded in a specific cultural context.

It follows then that translating naturally involves the transporting (carrying-over) of languages and their associated cultures to and recuperated by specific target reading constituencies. These constituencies have at their disposal established systems of representation, with norms and conventions for the production and consumption of meanings vis-à-vis people, objects and events. These

1

systems ultimately yield a master discourse through which identity and difference are marked and within which translating is carried out (Faiq, 2006a).
Summing up the shift in focus in translation studies that started in the
1980s, Hatim (2001, 83-4) writes:

> Under what may be termed 'the ideology of translation', translation theorists . . .
> have become interested in such aspects of the process as:
> • the choice of works to be translated (what is valued and what is excluded)
> • the power structure which controls the production and consumption of
>   translations
> • who has access to translation and who is denied access?
> • What is omitted, added or altered in seeking to control the message?

On the same point, Venuti (1995) posits that most Anglo-American translation projects have been invisible, producing transparent translations which
mirror the dominant culture. Related to invisibility is the issue of foreignizing, which Venuti defines as a

> strategic cultural intervention in the current state of world affairs, pitched
> against the hegemonic English-language nations and the unequal cultural ex-
> changes in which they engage their global others. (20)

Particularly in post-colonial societies, naturally related to translation are
national politics and language planning policies. Since the end of the First
World War, the application of the concept of self-determination has focused
on language as the main sign of belonging to warrant a community of speakers its own nation-state (Faiq, 1999). After the Second World War, in particular, the American and European obsession with monolingualism and the
one-nation, one-language perception has led to what Pennycook (1994) calls
a very particular Western cultural form. Significantly, Pennycook writes:

> [A]n almost unquestionable premise of Western linguistics has been that mono-
> lingualism is the norm both for communities of speakers and for individuals,
> with bi-or multilingualism taken as an exception and often stigmatised through
> its connections to minority groups, the Third World, and English as a Second
> Language Learners. (106)

Yet this single-minded approach of the West to issues of national identity
has rarely been granted to non-Western communities without provoking conflictual situations. This is because the West perceives the issue of the identity
of others as irrelevant or, at best, supportive to its own.

In this context of intercultural encounters, it is a truism to say that different cultures have historically represented each other in ways that have re-

flected the type of existing power relationships between them. Over the past three decades or so, post-colonial and translation studies, in particular, have contributed a great deal to the issues of the formation of cultural identities and/or representation of foreign cultures, what the late André Lefevere (1998) calls 'composing the other.'

The intercultural encounters that resulted in the great cultural shifts from one civilization to another have been made possible through translation, which, by conventional definition, deals with the 'beyond' (other) of one's immediate known world (self). But the 'beyond' is not easy to categorize or assimilate. In this regard, Bhabha (1994, 1) writes:

> The 'beyond' is neither a new horizon, nor a leaving behind of the past . . . beginnings and endings may be the sustaining myths of the middle years; but in the fin de siècle, we find ourselves in the moment of transit where space and time cross to produce complex figures of difference and identity, past and present, inside and outside, inclusion and exclusion. For there is a sense of disorientation, a disturbance of direction, in the 'beyond': an exploratory, restless movement caught so well in the French rendition of the words au-delà –

The beyond (in the eyes of Western cultures) has only been given some prominence when studies carried out in Canada, India, Latin America, as well as by scholars in Europe and the United States involved in post-colonial and multicultural disciplines, have pushed their respective disciplines, including translation studies, to consider different and challenging issues. In particular, the view of culture-modelling through translation has ushered in questions that cannot be adequately answered by the conventionalized, often evangelical, notions of equivalence and accuracy or the dichotomy 'sourceer' vs 'targeteer'. The focus has, then, shifted from (un)translatability to the cultural, political and economic ramifications; to what Hatim (2006) calls 'of-translation' as opposed to 'in-translation.'

So, in this culturally complex yet monoculturally global world, translation has assumed a unique position because of the widespread use of communication media, the politics of insurgent nationalisms (however defined and regardless of their bases), the emergence of international cultural organizations (UNESCO, for example), as well as the mingling of different ethnic, religious and linguistic communities in places previously deemed monocultural and primarily monolingual. Still and despite a relatively rapid integration within the global village, representations of some cultures, mainly through translation, have changed very little; rather they have remained fossilized, ethnocentrically oriented and guided by a particular master discourse.

Of these 'unfortunate' cultures, the Arab and Islamic cultures which, despite serious radical changes in their politics and socio-economic realities are still seen through the eyes of a fixed system of representation. Further, Arab and Islamic have been used as equal synonyms in Westerns cultures. Thomas (1998, 105) appropriately argues:

> The prevailing view of Arab culture as a mixture of the quaint, the barbarously primitive and the comfortably dependent, is to a large degree a product of those texts which have been selected for translation. One of the most frequently translated books is the *Thousand and One Nights*, which though not entirely Arab in origin supports what Said . . . has termed orientalism, that is a particularly patronizing, romantic, Western view of the East.

Centuries have gone by, but the Arab and Islamic worlds are still seen as stagnant entities with the dangerous addition in the last few years of new terms to the vocabulary of a master discourse that refuses to alter its system, so much so that Benjamin Barber (1992, 53), for example, posits two futures for the human race. One future is dictated by the forces of globalisation (Mc-World):

> by the onrush of economic and ecological forces that demand integration and uniformity and that mesmerize the world with fast music, fast computers, and fast food – with MTV, Macintosh, and McDonald's, pressing nations into one commercially homogeneous global network: one McWorld tied together by technology, ecology, communications and commerce.

The other future (McJihad) is driven by what he calls 'tribalism' that is seen as the extreme opposite of the former:

> a retribalization of large swaths of humankind by war and bloodshed: a threatened Lebanonization of national states in which culture is pitted against culture, people against people, tribe against tribe – a Jihad in the name of a hundred narrowly conceived faiths against every kind of interdependence, every kind of artificial social cooperation and civic mutuality.

The choice here of the words *Jihad* and *tribe* to describe the dangerous future for humanity immediately conjures up images of Arabs and Islam as the main causes of destructive nationalisms (tribalisms) that threaten the ways of life of the 'civilised' globalisation, which equates Western cultures.

Within this cultural framework, translation and the master discourse that underlies it regulate and animate the intercultural encounters between Arab/Islamic and Western cultures, leading to what Venuti (1996, 196) labels the violence of translation:

The violence of translation resides in its very purpose and activity: the reconstruction of the foreign text in accordance with values, beliefs, and representations that pre-exist in the target language, always configured in hierarchies of dominance and marginality, always determining the production, circulation, and reception of texts . . . Whatever difference the translation conveys is now imprinted by the target-language culture, assimilated to its positions of intelligibility, its canons and taboos, its codes and ideologies. The aim of translation is to bring back a cultural other as the same, the recognizable, even the familiar; and this aim always risks a wholesale domestication of the foreign text, often in highly self-conscious projects, where translation serves an imperialist appropriation of foreign cultures for domestic agendas, cultural, economic, political.

In this context and concerning the relationship between Arab(ic) and Islam and the West, the last two decades of the 20th century and specifically the first six years of the new century (after the events of 11 September 2001 in the USA), there has been an unprecedented use and abuse of stereotypes of Arabs and Islam. The same old story has been repeated over and over again, often with damaging consequences. That is, in the Western discourse, Arabs and Islam have become 'labels of primary potency' suppressing along the way the heterogeneity of these peoples and cultures. On the situation in the USA in the aftermath of the events, Edward Said (2002) comments:

[S]peaking Arabic or even reading an Arabic document in public is likely to draw unwelcome attention. And of course, the media have run far too many "experts" and "commentators" on terrorism, Islam, and the Arabs whose endlessly repetitive and reductive line is so hostile and so misrepresents our history, society and cultures.

Although historically the Arabs and Islam are the West's 'other' par excellence (Hentsch, 1992), little has been done to alter the nature of the stereotypes that regulate the discursive strategies in western discourses, including translation, about this other.

Notwithstanding the complexities of intercultural communication, the ethics of translation theoretically postulates that it should lead to a rapprochement between Bhabha's *au-delà*, the Arab/Muslim World, for our purpose in this volume, and the Western World, as the translator of this *au-delà*. And, since it covers the space-between cultures, translation could render the encounter less painful, less conflictual, less antagonistic, and less bloody. To achieve such a goal, translation traffic from Arabic into Western languages as well as translation from these languages into Arabic, need to reappraise and recast what the late André Lefevere (1999) calls 'the conceptual grid' and the 'textual grid' of translation or what Hatim (2001) labels 'the socio-textual' and 'socio-cultural' practices. In very general terms, the culture of translating and the translation of culture between Arabic and Western languages require a serious reconsideration on the basis that the in-between space need not come already formulated as a master discourse but as the space for negotiating a balanced understanding of the encounter through translation.

There have surely been genuine attempts by many Western journalists, critics and intellectuals to cut through stereotypical portrayals of the Arabs and Islam and to challenge and even disturb the master discourse and its norms for translation from Arabic and writing about the Arabs and Islam, but they are usually overwhelmed by the ubiquity of the dominant discourse that provides the frames within which representations take place.

A better understanding of the ways in which discourses operate might contribute to more efficient self-monitoring on the part of producers of master discourses and might lead to making translation a true process of intercultural understanding rather than reinforcing existing representations and images of one culture for another. This can be achieved through a cross-cultural appraisal of the discourses underlying translation and translating with a view to better understanding the issues of identity (self and other), translation enterprise (patronage, agencies, translators) and norms of representation (master discourse).

Like nearly half of the contemporary world that has been profoundly affected by colonialism, Arab and Muslim countries have struggled to strike a balance between the desire to join Western modernity (and its post-modernity) and the demand for the recreation of a tradition free from colonial taint. Translation has pride of place in this struggle. But the discourse of translation from Arabic still haunts any fair intercultural exchange. It seems the West has already decided that Arab and Islamic cultures have nothing of substance to offer modern history. Translation from it, therefore, remains prisoner of nineteenth century images and representations.

To conclude this chapter, the late André Lefevere (1998, 12-13), quoted verbatim, examines the very issues discussed here: how different cultural traditions view translation and the process of translating.

Different cultures have tended to take translation for granted, or rather, different cultures have taken the technique of translating that was current at a given time in their evolution for granted and equated it with the phenomenon of translation as such. Histories of translation in the West have shown increasingly that the technique of translating in Western cultures has changed repeatedly over the centuries, and that what was accepted as 'obvious' at one particular time was, in fact, little more than a passing phase. The important point is that shifts and changes in the technique of translating did not occur at random. Rather, they were intimately linked with the way in which different cultures, at different times, came to terms with the phenomenon of translation, with the challenge posed by the existence of the Other and the need to select from a number of possible strategies for dealing with that Other. We are, therefore, finally beginning to see different methods of translating as well as different approaches to translational practice as contingent, not eternal, as changeable, not fixed, because we are beginning to recognize that they have, indeed, changed over the centuries. Paradoxically, once it is accepted that translation is contingent, it becomes possible to highlight the central position it has always occupied in the development, indeed the very definition of cultures. That contingency is even easier to see when two different traditions are compared. Such a comparison may, I believe, shed light not just on the two traditions, but ultimately also on the phenomenon of translation itself.

If we are to examine translation projects and practices, we ought to carefully consider the culture of doing translation simply because the culture of translation ultimately guides and regulates the translation of culture.

Chapter Two

The Master Discourse of Translation

CULTURE, LANGUAGE AND TRANSLATION

The two fundamental components of translation are culture and language, and given that these two, separate or together, have preoccupied researchers for decades, the search is still on for comprehensive definitions and/or theories of both. Because it brings the two together, translation is by necessity a multi-faceted, multi-problematic process with different manifestations and realizations in different cultures/traditions of the world.

In general terms, culture can be defined as shared knowledge: what the members of a particular community ought to know in order to act and react in particular ways and interpret their experience in distinctive ways. Culture then involves the totality of attitudes towards the world, towards events, other cultures and peoples and the manner in which the attitudes are mediated (Fairclough, 1995; Scollon, 1998). In other words, culture refers to beliefs and value systems tacitly assumed to be collectively shared by particular social groups as well as to the positions taken by producers and receivers of texts, including translations, during the mediation process facilitated by language. Language is the system that provides its users with the tools to realize their culture. The intrinsic relationship between culture and language is expressed by Bassnett (1998a, 81) in the following simple way: "Try as I may, I cannot take language out of culture or culture out of language."

The norms of producing, classifying, interpreting, and circulating texts within the sociocultural contexts of one language tend to remain in force when approaching texts transplanted through translation from other sociocultural contexts written in other languages. As with native texts, the reception process of translated texts is determined more by the shared knowledge of the translating community and its language, than by what the translated texts themselves contain. But while languages are generally prone to change over time (phonologically, morphologically, syntactically and semantically) cultures do not change in the same way. Overall, cultures remain by and large captive of their past or even pasts. Edward Said (1993, 1) succinctly argues:

> Appeals to the past are among the commonest of strategies in interpretations of the present. What animates such appeals is not only disagreement about what happened in the past and what the past was, but uncertainty about whether the past really is past, over and concluded, or whether it continues, albeit in different forms, perhaps. This problem animates all sorts of discussions—about influence, about blame and judgement, about present actualities and future priorities.

It is in these pasts that cultures usually reside and, even if the colors, shapes and formulations of these residences change, the spirit of cultures changes little or not at all. When cultures cross and mingle through translation, these pasts come face to face and a struggle for power and influence becomes inevitable. Old formulations and modes of mediation appear on the surface and their realization is made possible by language.

The last three decades or so have also witnessed an increased interest in considering language from the perspective of critical discourse analysis, which basically examines how the use of language, as discourse, is invested with ideologies in the production, circulation and/or challenging of existing stereotypes or power relationships (interculturally and intraculturally) between communities of the same language or communities of different languages. Within such a context, language is seen as a systematic and consistent body of representations that reflect specific social practices from particular points of view.

According to van Dijk (1993, 253), critical discourse analysis involves the multidisciplinary exploration of the "intricate relationships between text, talk, social cognition, power, society, and culture."

The characterization of language use as such leads to the production of a master discourse through which users establish hierarchies of meaning and 'chains of signs' with particular modes of representations (Bhabha, 1994). But a master discourse does not normally reflect reality; instead it makes use of language in such a way that reality is constructed, as Bakhtin (1981, 342) writes:

> The authoritative word is located in a distanced zone, organically connected with a past that is felt to be hierarchically higher . . . It is a prior discourse. (cited in Conklin, 1997: 239).

Within critical discourse analysis, any discourse is always under two types of pressure: *centripetal* and *centrifugal* (Bakhtin, 1994; 1986; 1981). Centripetal pressures

> follow from the need in producing a text to draw upon given conventions, of two main classes; a language, and an order of discourse – that is, a historically particular structuring of discursive (text-producing) practices. (Fairclough, 1995: 7)

Centrifugal pressures on discourse relate generally to the discursive choices to serve particular situations. Fairclough (Ibid, 7) expounds: "Centrifugal pressures come from the specificity of particular situations of text-production."

Of the two types, centripetal pressures are more ideologically oriented and tend to map out the way for decisions to deal with the centrifugal ones.

Along a similar line of inquiry, Bourdieu postulates that the dialectic of dominating and dominated agents yields a particular position for the delimitation and characterization of *fields*, *habitus* and ultimately an *illusio*. For Bourdiou (1993), texts are produced within particular fields as cultural goods for particular social groups by agents whose actions stem from interests that proceed from their habitus, that is, the given society. When the cultural production of a particular social group achieves the status of domination, its master discourse, with all its centripetal pressures, creates the *illusio* that becomes synonymous with a fixed mode of cultural production.

Through adherence to the requirements and constraints of a master discourse that underpins translation, source texts become situated into ways of representation (chains of signs) ingrained in the shared experience and institutional norms of the translating community or communities (self, selves, us). Source texts and their associated peoples are transformed from certain specific signs into signs whose typifications translators and others involved in the translation enterprise claim to know (Conklin, 1997).

As the antonym of the self (the translating community or culture), the other (otherness, them, the translated community or culture) is used to refer to all peoples the self perceives as mildly or radically different. Historically, the other and otherness have been feared than appreciated with the exception of the phenomenon of exoticism, where the other, though often misunderstood and misrepresented, is perceived as foreign, alien and different but at the same time strangely attractive (O'Barr, 1994).

In intercultural contacts through translation, otherness is measured according to a scale of allowed choices within the master discourse: when the other is feared, the lexical strategies one expects are those that realize hierarchy, subordination and dominance in a power relationship. When such a situation arises, otherness can, and often does, lead to the establishment of stereotypes, which usually come accompanied by existing representations that reinforce the ideas behind them.

Some critics see stereotypes as complex, ambivalent, contradictory modes of representation, and as 'anxious as they are assertive.' Stereotypes tend to dehumanize certain groups, making it easier for those formulating and using them to control, appropriate and subvert the stereotyped other while minimizing the complex web of 'emotions of guilt and shame' (Bhabha, 1994).

Within this context, the representation of others, mainly external others, through translation is a powerful strategy of exclusion used by a self as 'normal and moral' (Said, 1995). This exclusion is also accompanied by an including process of some accepted members from the other as long as these accepted individuals adopt and adapt to the system underlying the master discourse and its associated representational system and ideology of the accepting self (Faiq, 2000a).

The application of critical discourse analysis approaches and the concept of the master discourse, as expounded here, aims to examine how translation, as the intercultural communication, is shaped by ideologies and cultures and how, as such, translation "contributes to the perpetuation or subversion of particular discourses" (Olk, 2002: 101).

Approached from this perspective, translation yields sites for examining a plethora of issues: race, gender, colonialism, post-colonialism, publishing policies, censorship, and cultural identity. In this web, all parties involved in the translation enterprise, from the choice of texts for translation to discursive decisions, tend to assume what their readers want to know about foreign lands and peoples. In this regard, translation

> wields enormous power in constructing representations of foreign cultures. The selection of foreign texts and the development translation strategies can establish peculiarly domestic canons for foreign literatures, canons that conform to domestic aesthetic values and therefore reveal exclusions and admissions, centres and peripheries that deviate from those current in the foreign language. (Venuti, 1998: 67)

Along the same line of argument, Venuti (1998, 1996, 1995) has further argued that the very purpose and activity of translation represents violence. Reiterating views of many researchers like Walter Benjamins and postulating the concepts of *domestication* and *foreignization*, Venuti further argues that the Anglo-American translation tradition, in particular, has had a normalizing and naturalizing effect—that is the killing and negation of otherness and cultural differences. Such an effect has deprived source text producers of their voice and culminated in the re-expression of foreign cultural values in terms of what is familiar to the dominant Western culture.

Venuti discusses the linguistic hegemony of English in terms of the *invisibility* of the translator. Invisibility is apparent when translations yield fluent readability and feel like originals rather than imitations (translations). Invisibility requires a great deal of manipulation on the part of the translator because as Venuti (1995, 2) says:

> The more fluent the translation, the more invisible the translator, and, presumably, the more visible the writer or meaning of the foreign text.

Invisible translators, accordingly, produce *transparent* translations, which mirror the dominant culture. Related to invisibility is the issue of foreignizing, which Venuti (Ibid, 20) defines as

> a strategic cultural intervention in the current state of world affairs, pitched against the hegemonic English-language nations and the unequal cultural exchanges in which they engage their global others.

THE MASTER DISCOURSE
OF TRANSLATION FROM ARABIC

Particularly since the 1980s, translation studies has been extended to consider different and challenging issues. In particular, the view of culture-modelling through translation has ushered in questions that cannot be adequately answered by the conventionalized notions of equivalence, faithfulness and accuracy. The focus has shifted from (un)translatability to the cultural, political and economic ramifications of translation. It should be noted here that this shift has largely been precipitated by work in orientalism, post-colonial and cultural studies, and by the questioning of the transparent and fluent strategies and practices of translating others.

The treatment of translation from an ideological point of view in terms of power relationships, identity formation, self and other is labeled invisibility by Venuti (1995), appropriation by Kuhiwczak (1990), and subversion by Carbonell (1996), to name but a few examples.

Regardless of how different researchers define their labels and terms, the general reference is to the way translation is carried out under the pressures of a hegemonic consideration of all that is other by the translating cultures. Kuhiwczak discusses the appropriated translation of central European literature into English, Venuti discusses invisible translations of Italian and Japanese works into American English and Carbonell examines the ways Arabic texts have been subverted through translation into mainstream European languages, in general, and Spanish, in particular.

In translation, invisibility, appropriation and subversion can all be subsumed under *manipulation*, which not only distorts original texts but also leads to the influencing of target readers. Carbonell (1996), for example, reports that in his comments on Burton's translation of the *Arabian Nights*, Byron Farwell (1963/1990, 366) wrote:

> The great charm of Burton's translation, viewed as literature, lies in the veil of romance and exoticism he cast over the entire work. He tried hard to retain the flavour of oriental quaintness and naivete of the medieval Arab by writing as the Arab would have written in English.

Such views of translation and of the source language and its associated culture as well as of the readers of the target text (translation), lead to translations that imply the production of subverted texts (translations) at all levels,

> not only the source text, but also the target context experience the alteration infused by the translation process when their deeper implications are thus revealed. (Carbonell, 1996: 93)

This alteration ultimately leads to manipulations of the target text through the process of translation, thus regulating and/or satisfying pre-existing and expected responses of and/or sought by the receivers of the translations.

Starting from the premise that cultural and translation studies deal with the conditions of knowledge production in one culture and the way this knowledge is interpreted and relocated according to knowledge production in another culture, translation from Arabic into Western languages has been in the main carried out through a master discourse that is regulated by specific *topos* (singular: *topoi*). Topos are primary stereotypes that constitute reservoirs of ideas and core images (preserved in the collective memory of the translating culture) from which most representations and translations generate their specific centripetal pressures that dictate the discoursal features used in the writing of translations or other texts about the source culture (Karim, 1997; Said, 1997).

Of specific importance, translation from Arabic has followed representational strategies within an established framework of institutions with its own vocabulary and scripts (Said, 1993). In this framework of relations of power and knowledge, the West, satisfied and content with its own representations, has not deemed it necessary to appreciate appropriately, through translation, the literatures and respective cultures of these peoples, except for texts that fit the requirements of the master discourse of the translating culture (there are, of course, exceptions but they do not affect mainstream trends).

Reporting on personal experience of translating contemporary Arabic literature into English, Peter Clark (1997, 109) writes:

I wanted . . . to translate a volume of contemporary Syrian literature. I . . . thought the work of 'Abd al-Salam al-'Ujaili was very good and well worth putting into English. 'Ujaili is a doctor in his seventies who has written poetry, criticism, novels and short stories. In particular his short stories are outstanding. Many are located in the Euphrates valley and depict the tensions of individuals coping with politicisation and the omnipotent state . . . .. I proposed to my British publisher a volume of 'Ujaili's short stories. The editor said, "There are three things wrong with the idea. He's male. He's old and he writes short stories. Can you find a young female novelist?" Well, I looked into women's literature and did translate a novel by a woman writer even though she was and is in her eighties.

This account shows that translation from Arabic into mainstream European languages is essentially still seen as an exotic voyage carried out through a weighty component of representation in the target culture.

In this target culture, the objective knowledge of the original language and its culture is substantially altered by a dialectic of attraction and repulsion (Said, 1993). The *Arabian Nights* (a title preferred for its exotic and salacious resonance to the original *A Thousand and One Nights*), for instance, is more famous in the West than in the Arab East. Further, the proportion of books written about the Arab and Islamic worlds in Western languages is greatly disproportionate to the small number of books translated from its literatures.

This particular situation may have contributed to the low status of translation in the Arab world (Faiq, 2000b). Statistics reported by Venuti (1995, 14) show that of all translations worldwide for the years 1982, 1983 and 1984, translations from Arabic were 298, 322 and 536 respectively. Compared with translations from Spanish or Hungarian or even classical Greek and Latin, one can easily notice the insignificance of the number of translations from Arabic; an alive-and-kicking language in today's world. Translations from Spanish, Hungarian and classical Greek and Latin were 715, 847, 839; 703, 665, 679; and 839, 1116, 1035 for the three years respectively. Edward Said (1995, 97) aptly remarks on such a situation:

> For all the major world literatures, Arabic remains relatively unknown and unread in the West, for reasons that are unique, even remarkable, at a time when tastes here for the non-European are more developed than ever before and, even more compelling, contemporary Arabic literature is at a particularly interesting juncture.

Despite the interesting juncture, despite excellent literary works and despite a Nobel Prize in literature (awarded to the Egyptian writer Naguib Mahfouz in 1988), there seems to be a general 'embargo' except for texts that reiterate the usual clichés about 'Islam,' violence, sensuality, and so forth' (Said 1995, 99).

In the discourse of translation, the Arab/Islamic world has become a homogeneous entity (sign) invisibly constructed, defined and stereotyped. In this context, translation becomes a significant technology of domination and as a means of improving the 'debased' native texts through translation (recall Byron Farwell). This in turn ultimately leads to the conclusion that translation also becomes the site of conflictual relationships of power and struggle between the cultures being translated and those doing the translating, with potentially dire consequences and accusations and counter accusations of misrepresentation and subversion.

The basis in most representations of all that is Arab and Islamic lies in the Western obsession with fixed texts generated from master discourses and the fixation with the mechanisms of this fixedness, which all non-Western cultures are presumed to lack. Translating from Arabic, with specific traditions for the production, reception and circulation of texts into fixed texts has meant taking liberties, being invisible, violent, appropriationist and subverter to shift them into mainstream world culture and literature of fixed texts: specific canons of production that also stand as signs of universalism and humanism. Texts produced by the other can be accepted by the self as long as they conform to existing norms expected and accepted by the self (Asad, 1995).

When Arab writers like Munif, the superb critic of modern and post-modern Arab societies, are translated into English, critics either ignore or denigrate their writings. Dallal (1998, 8) quotes the critic John Updike's remark about Munif's outstanding *Cities of Salt*:

> It is unfortunate . . . that Mr Munif . . . appears to be . . . insufficiently Westernized to produce a narrative that feels much like what we call a novel.

Such an attitude stems from the one-sided, still current stereotypical ideology based on universalism, unitarism, and the homogeneity of human nature from a particular perspective. This ideology marginalizes and excludes the distinctive and unique characteristics of Arab societies and their discursive traditions. What Updike is saying is that the West needs to satisfy itself that it knows its natives: it is others who should adapt to its norms in order to be welcomed as members of universalism and world culture and literature.

The western centric assumptions about others—races, nationalities, literatures—has provided the site for critiques of representations, language and ideological control towards writers from places like the Arab world. These assumptions return time and again to haunt the production, reception and circulation of Arabic texts, and in turn complicate the issue of translation (Jacquemond, 1992).

True, the 1980s and 1990s witnessed a considerable opening up by Western cultures and societies onto *Third World* peoples, cultures and texts (Latin America, for example), but the literatures of the Arab-Islamic world have remained generally marginalized, despite the enormous and persistent attention—almost hysteria—accorded to Arabs and to Islam. Translation from Arabic still proceeds along familiar and established scripts whereby

> stereotyping, strategies of signification and power: the network in which a culture is fashioned does appear as a texture of signs linked by endless connotations and denotations, a meaning system of inextricable complexity that is reflected, developed and recorded in the multifarious act of writing. (Carbonell, 1996: 81)

In his translation of Naguib Mahfouz's novel *Yawma qutila z-za'iim* (The Day the Leader was Killed/Assassinated), André Miquel, for example, explains in his foreword to the French-language reader that he kept footnotes (footnotes being interventions by the translator) to the very minimum. Yet Jacquemond (1992) counted 54 footnotes in a 77 page translation. What transpires is that the translator-cum-orientalist expert assumes total ignorance on the part of readers, and proceeds to guide them through assumed authoritative knowledge of an unfathomable world where backwardness and the assassination of peace-makers are the norms. But this would be acceptable compared with Edward Fitzgerald's infamous comment on the liberties he allowed himself to take with his version of *The Rubaiyat of Omar Khayam*, which, according to him, needed some art to shape them (Bassnett, 1998b). Concerning these same issues, Thomas (1998, 104-5) writes:

> Arab culture . . . vis-à-vis the West, has largely been positioned through the selection of translation material. The prevailing view of Arab culture as a mixture of the quaint, the barbarously primitive and the comfortably dependent, is to a large degree a product of those texts which have been selected for translation . . . In this regard it is interesting to consider Naguib Mahfoudh – the only Arab writer to have been given the full western seal of approval through his winning of the Nobel Prize. He worked as a censor throughout the Nasser and Sadat eras, eras not noted for liberal attitudes to the arts or critical awarness. He also appeared on Israeli television on a number of occasions supporting a pro-western position. Despite what one may think of the literary merits of his work . . . the fact remains that nearly all of his work has been translated, which compares very favourably with translations of other Arab writers who have been much more critical of the West.

So, Arabic literary texts are rarely chosen for translation for their innovative approaches or for their socio-political perspectives, rather texts chosen are recognizable as conforming to the master discourse of writing about and representing Arabs, Arab culture and Islam. This situation has led many Arab writers to write in and for translation – writing in Arabic but with an eye on the readers of translations into Western languages.

Discussing the discursive strategies of the female Arab writer, Hanan al-Shaykh in her Arabic novel *Women of Sand and Myrrh*, Dallal (1998, 8), for example, appropriately writes:

> That *Women of Sand and Myrrh* was written specifically for English-speaking audiences is clear in the opening chapter. References specific to Western culture which would be unfamiliar to Arabs go unexplained, whereas references to customs or practices specific to Arab contexts are consistently accompanied by explanations. Suha explains why "the [imported] soft toys and dolls had all been destroyed" by the authorities: "every one that was meant to be a human being or animal or bird [was confiscated] since it was not permissible to produce distortions of God's creatures". This explanation of a particular interpretation of Islam (or outright fabrication, as most Arab Muslims would believe) used by the Gulf regimes would need no explanation for Arab audiences. However, the narrators' references to "Barbie dolls and Snoopies and Woodstocks" would not be recognized by most in the Arab world, and yet are left without explanation.

Along similar lines, Nawal al-Saadawi, the most translated Arab writer today after Naguib Mahfouz, provides another example. Her fame in the West does not stem from her attempts as a writer who critically assesses social practices, particularly women's issues, in the Arab world but primarily from her accounts of clitoridectomy: accounts in demand in the West.

This has led Saadawi to tailor her writings in response to the pressures and appeals of the Western marketplace. A further example is the novel *In the Eye of the Sun* (written in English by the Arab female writer Ahdaf Sueif), which has been hailed a great work because primarily the story at the level of sex and shopping is an absorbing one.

For the norms of the master discourse of cultural representation, including writing about and translation from as well mass media portrayals of Arabs and Islam in the West, Karim (1997) provides striking examples of headlines in American magazines and newspapers across the political spectrum. The few examples listed below, self-explanatory, demonstrate adherence to a master discourse of representation that usually portrays the over one billion Muslims of the world as a monolith.

- Muslim rage
- an angry faith
- dark side of Islam
- the Vatican's dark marriage to Islam
- The Crescent of Crisis
- Moslems battle police in Malaysia Bloodbath
- Egyptian Police, Moslems Clash

- Algerian Muslims Seek Power
- Islamic death threat
- Islamic suicide mission
- Islamic powder keg

As argued elsewhere in this book, the self (the translating culture) tends to accept some individuals from the other (the translated culture) as long as they do not challenge the self's master discourse and its norms of handling and representing that other. With regard to translation from and writing about the Arab World and Islam, the reception of Arabs and Muslims writing in Western languages, particularly English and French, has depended on the extent to which these authors adopt and adapt to existing norms of translating from and representing the Arab World and Islam. What is known as Arabic Literature in French (ALF) is an interesting case in point (see chapter 3 in this volume).

Referring to the notions of transparency, invisibility and fluency in translation, Bassnett (1998b) appropriately argues that translation projects guided by such concepts always favour the target readers, so much so that the source text, its culture and readers become insignificant. In the case of translation from Arabic, the target readers are mainly Anglo-Americans but also French, Spanish, and other Europeans (Carbonell, 1996). But this is not entirely new it has been noted in the history of relations between East and West. In this regard, Bassnett (1998b, 78) writes:

> This tendency in English began to develop in the nineteenth century and accelerated with the translation of texts from non-European languages, from literatures that, as Edward Fitzgerald remarked in his infamous comment on the liberties he had allowed himself to take with his version of the *Rubaiyat of Omar Khayam*, 'really need a little art to shape them'. Currently, reaction in the postcolonial world to the colonizing impact of translation is so strongly felt that there are those who argue that western cultures, particularly English speaking ones, should NOT translate other literatures at all.

Bassnett hastens to point out that this is not a position with which she agrees, but one with which she sympathizes. Others, particularly Venuti (1995; 1998), have set out to redress the balance by embarking on their own translation projects whereby the target language, American English in particular, is manipulated to ensure the original text and its culture survive the translating act. But any translation is carried out under constraints, which include manipulation of power relations between dominated and dominating, and ultimately lead to the construction of images of the translated cultures in ways that preserve and/or expand the hegemony of the translating culture (Lefevere, 1990).

In translating from Arabic or writing about its culture, the images construct the other in ways that are recognizable to the self, as authentic within the framework of a particular poetics and ideology – a particular master discourse. The late Andre Lefevere (1995, 465) succinctly wrote:

> A literature . . . can be described as a system, embedded in the environment of a civilization/culture/society, call it what you will. The system is not primarily demarcated by a language, or an ethnic group, or a nation, but by a poetics, a collection of devices available for use by writers at a certain moment in time . . . The environment exerts control over the system, by means of patronage. Patronage combines both an ideological and an economic component. It tries to harmonize the system with other systems it has to co-exist with in the wider environment – or simply imposes a kind of harmony.

In the case of translation from Arabic, Levefere's last argument applies wholesale. For centuries, Arabic has been made to conform to the prevailing systems at work in the West. Moreover and interestingly, the system, despite the rapid changes Western societies have witnessed, not least in terms of tolerance of others, multiculturalism and multiligualism, translation from Arabic and writings in Western languages about the Arabs and Islam have remained prisoner of the same discursive, poetic and ideological framework; reminiscent of Fitzgerald's comments. The Arab world and Islam are still translated/represented through monolingual eyes, as Dallal (1998, 8) comments:

> One of the ironies about multiculturalism is how parochial it is. Despite ever increasing globalism, multiculturalism remains largely monolingual and limited to American culture: consider the absence of interest in Arabic literature and culture in Western Europe and the United States, despite the enormous and persistent attention paid to the Arab world and to Islam.

Arab culture and Islam, distanced by time, space and language(s), are usually carried over into a Western tradition as an originary moment and imagined within a master discourse of translation that is full of ready-made stereotypes and clichés (Said, 1997; Layoun, 1995; Faiq, 2003). This situation has persisted despite the fact that the Arab world is a melting pot of nations, languages, dialects, constituencies, religious practices, and ideologies; a world that has also seen most forms of appropriation and subversion, including physical violence through many wars in history (note all the wars during the first six years of this century alone).

It can perhaps be argued that such attitudes of the West towards the Arab world, through translation and representation, can be rationalized on the basis that two different cultures with two separate pasts have clashed, and continue to do so. The Europeans colonized the Arab lands for decades, and the post-colonial situation is different only in terms of the fact that after the Second World War, the United States became in many ways the guardian and custodian of the Arab world. Given such a premise, one can argue that manipulatory and subversive cultural representations of one side to the other may be taken as part of the scheme of history. After all, without such clashes, manipulations and subversions, history would not be history. The same discursive strategies still prevail, however.

The representations of Arabs and Islam by and/or for the West are not just accounts of different places, cultures and societies, but more importantly they are projections of the West's own fears and desires masqueraded as objective knowledge: consider the issue of the *Hijaab* (head scarf) of Muslim women and bearded Arab-looking men.

For all post-colonial communities, and particularly the Arabs, the drive in literature, politics, and translation towards national identity has centered on language mainly because, as During (1995, 125) argues, within the context of post-modernity, identity is barely available elsewhere. So, in the post-colonial Arab world, the return to Arabic is still a political, cultural, and literary question, because the choice of the language, in the material sense at least, is a choice of identity. To continue using French, English, or Spanish calls forth a problem of identity, which is then thrown into mimicry and ambivalence (Bhabha, 1994; Faiq, 2000a, b).

The project of most post-colonial Arab writers has been, and is still, to interrogate both western and indigenous discourses by exploding and confounding different symbolic worlds and separate systems, through translation and other forms of writing. However, there are a number of Arabs, to whom I refer here as *native foreigners*, to use Beaugrande (2006) terms, who can easily be categorized as belonging to those Westerners labeled by Edward Said as orientalists. The difference between the two groups is that, while Said's orientalists can be accommodated as belonging to a particular culture that is not Arab/Islamic, our *native foreigners* come from the indigenous Arab/Islamic environment, and yet adopt the same translation (representation) as that developed and sustained by Said's orientalists (see chapters 3 and 4 in this volume for a discussion of these issues).

The authoritarian relationships between translators and what they deem inferior source cultures was compatible with the rise and spread of colonialism. But though colonialism in its conventional sense at least is no more, the authoritarian relationships still persist, particularly vis-à-vis the Arabs and Islam leading to what Said (1997, 163) calls cultural antipathy:

Today Islam is defined negatively as that with which the West is radically at odds, and this tension establishes a framework radically limiting knowledge of

Islam. So long as this framework stands, Islam, as a vitally lived experience for Muslims, cannot be known.

The outcome of this cultural antipathy towards the Arabs and Islam is manifest in the minuscule translations from Arabic except, of course, for those texts that further reinforce the privileged representations that have acquired the status of facts. The discursive strategies and transparencies in translating all that is Arab and Islamic tend to refer to static and timeless societies and peoples, which are turned into naturalized and dehistoricized images within a particular master discourse. As Spivak (1985, 253-54) puts it:

> No perspective *critical* of imperialism can turn the Other into a self, because the project of imperialism has always already historically refracted what might have been the absolutely Other into a domesticated Other that consolidates the imperialist fracture or discontinuity, covered over by an alien legal system masquerading as Law as such, an alien ideology established as only truth, as a set of human sciences busy establishing the native 'as self-consolidating Other.' (emphasis in the original)

Translation from Arabic still makes immediate use of the fixed structures and vocabulary that have persisted for many centuries, whereby Arabs and Islam are not only normally translated into established discursive strategies and a range of allusiveness for the target language readers, but also into the very norms of choosing what to translate, ways of publishing and expected reviewing methods.

> [T]he power of translation to (re)constitute and cheapen foreign texts, to trivialize and exclude foreign cultures, and thus potentially to figure in racial discrimination and ethnic violence, international political confrontations, terrorism, war. (Venuti 1996, 196)

The points in the quote apply to translation from Arabic. Hatim (2006), for example, shows how the semiotic mishandling, most certainly intended, of simple words in Arabic or Farsi triggers the images of violence, terrorism and fundamentalism; labels among many that are pre-texts but serve as pretexts reserved for the Arabs and Islam (see Zlateva, 1990 for a discussion of the notions of pre-text and pretext in translation).

It is anticipated that as counter attacks, post-colonial literary and translation projects in the Arab and Muslim worlds would aim at valorizing and enriching native cultures in order to improve their production, reception and circulation systems. Fanon (1961, 37-8) summarizes the natural process native intellectuals would normally go through to the post-colonial via the colonial phase:

The colonialist bourgeoisie had in fact deeply implanted in the minds of the colonized intellectual that the essential qualities remain eternal in spite of all the blunders men may make: the essential qualities of the West, of course. The native intellectual accepted the cogency of these ideas and deep down in his brain you could find a vigilant sentinel ready to defend the Greco-Latin pedestal. Now it so happens that during the struggle for liberation, at the moment that the native intellectual comes into touch again with his people, this artificial sentinel is turned into dust. All the Mediterranean values,—the triumph of the human individual of clarity and beauty – become lifeless, colourless knick-knacks. All those speeches seem like collections of dead words; those values which seemed to uplift the soul are revealed as worthless, simply because they have nothing to do with the concrete conflict in which the people is engaged.

Fanon's arguments are appropriate enough where the return to pre-colonial language(s), traditions and ideology are seen as resistance tools for the refusal of all that is colonial. But, as During (1995) argues, post-colonial communities usually suffer from a deep sense of defeat by the former colonial powers, and that freedom is often seen as the enemy's gift, regardless of how its achievement is portrayed by the post-colonial ideologies of the new native order. Post-colonial literary and translation projects need to come into their own, not only in terms of how many great works are imitated or translated, but in terms of establishing a whole apparatus capable of supporting the projects: a publishing industry, including magazines, journals, and critics; a critical use of language(s), and understanding of norms and values; a particularized context of myths about the past and the present; a determination for continuity; and above all, a readership (Gray, 1984).

Particularly over the last 30 years or so, the cultural encounter between Arabic and its world and the West has witnessed an unprecedented use and abuse of stereotypes, often with damaging consequences on both sides, with the eastern side suffering most. There have been genuine attempts by many Westerners to challenge and even disturb their own cultures' master discourses and their norms for translation from Arabic and writing about its world, but they are usually in the minority.

A better understanding of the ways in which discourses operate and how they become master discourses might contribute to more efficient self-monitoring on the part of producers of master discourses, and might lead to making translation a true process of intercultural understanding rather than reinforcing existing representations and images of one culture about another. This can be achieved through a cross-cultural appraisal of the discourses underlying translation and translating with a view to better understanding the issues of identity (self and other), translation enterprise (patronage, agencies, translators) and norms of representation (master discourse). If we are to examine the process of intercultural communication through translation, we ought to carefully consider the culture of doing translation since the culture of translation guides and regulates the translation of culture, and ultimately the cultural *betwixt* (the space between traveled by texts in the process of intercultural translation).

Chapter Three

A Case of Pseudo-translation

PSEUDO-TRANSLATION

In translation studies, the issue of a translation not being a translation has generally been discussed under the concept of pseudo-translation: a text falsely claimed as a translation. The label pseudo-translation is used to refer to a text created from scratch by an author who claims to have produced no more than a translation, often attributing his/her text to a figure from another culture.

Toury (1995), for example, posits that in seeking to convince readers that the pseudo-translation is a genuine translation, its author takes into account the expectations of the readership. But since pseudo-translation covers anything that is not real, then even a 'true' translation—in terms of the existence of a source text—may also be easily labeled pseudo-translation, particularly if it serves no purpose of translation as intercultural communication.

Pseudo-translations or fictitious translations and their variations form an interesting aspect in translation studies that has not been given the critical attention it deserves. In a rare article on this topic, Bassnett (1998c) lists four major types of pseudo-translation.

INAUTHENTIC SOURCE

The inauthentic source is a device used mostly in stories whereby readers, as Bassnett (Ibid.) argues, collude from the outset with the translator – author – that a source exists behind the claimed translation. On the status of this type of fictitious translation, Bassnett (Ibid. 30) concludes:

> The question is, however, whether we may call this kind of text a translation, for although it presupposes an original somewhere else and claims to be a

rendering of that original, is not a single text but a body of material in several languages.

SELF-TRANSLATION

Self-translation introduces another dimension to the question of whether a claimed translation is really a translation. Bassnett (1998c) cites the example of Samuel Beckett, who famously wrote in both French and English, claiming at times to have translated his own texts.

In self-translation, the translators-cum-authors find themselves in a complex position. They try to manipulate the position that readers of the translation are assumed to occupy. They do so by blurring their reading position as translators and their position as authors of the original, while all the time laying claim to objectivity in translation. Often translators-cum-authors subjectively manipulate readers to position themselves where they want; not where their status as readers would normally allow them. In such cases, the translators-cum-authors blur the distances between author, reader and translator, with the ultimate goal of steering readers into a particular reading position.

As Bassnett (Ibid, 31) writes, the moment we are told that a text is actually a translation of an original text by the translator,

> we are thrown up against the problem of the 'authenticity' of the 'original'. One solution to the dilemma is to deny the existence of any original, and consequently to deny the existence of a translation, assuming instead that we have two versions of the same text that simply happen to have been written by the same author in different languages.

INVENTING TRANSLATION

Invented translation applies when authors invent originals for their own 'texts-cum-translations-invented.' Bassnett (1998c) cites the example of Francis Burton who claimed to have translated a Persian poem, when he actually wrote the whole text himself. Perhaps not sure how his own writing would be received by his British readers, Burton resorted to claiming translation rather than authorship.

Claiming their own texts to be no more than mere translations, allows some writers to escape the usual scrutiny of critics and readers but can also be a way of importing ideologies and views that are not easily accepted by the culture of these authors. In the following rather long but illuminating and fitting quote, Amit-Kochavi (2004, 56-7) shows how invented sources have been used by Israeli authors for particular political and ideological purposes.

Cases of pseudo-translation are well-known in other instances of intercultural contact (Toury, 1995:40-52) where the claimed source culture is usually considered as superior to the presumed target culture, so that it is worth presenting one's own work as coming from a more prestigious source. In the case of Arabic and Hebrew, however, Arabic culture is generally considered by Hebrew culture as either non-existent or inferior, so there was no obvious gain to be made from pretending to have borrowed from it. What, then, made Israeli Jewish writers hide behind an invented Arab identity in spite of these unfavourable circumstances? The two cases described here provide two different answers to this question.

In the first case, Yisrael Eliraz, a playwright noted for the opera libretti he writes to the music of Israeli composer Joseph Tal, invented an Arab persona by the name of Georges Matiyya Ibrahim, a Palestinian born in Bethlehem and studying and living in Paris. Ibrahim presumably wrote poems in French, in which he expressed his longing for his home town and the beautiful landscapes of the West Bank, and sent them to Eliraz, with whom he had studied in Paris, who translated them into Hebrew. The pseudo-translations were produced and published over a long period (1979-1987) during which Eliraz also published a volume of poetry in his own name, the similarity of which to the presumably 'translated' poems aroused no suspicion. They were applauded for their beauty and elaborate style and published in several prominent literary magazines as well as two collections (1980/1988; 1984). When Eliraz finally admitted the truth he was interviewed by both the Hebrew and Arabic press about his reasons for the pretence. He explained that he had long been known as playwright and librettist, so when he attempted to write poetry he did not want to be judged by his past achievements. Therefore he chose to hide behind a persona with which he shared many biographical details—Georges Matiyya Ibrahim was a real Palestinian student he had known in Paris. Eliraz's explanation provides an excuse for hiding behind a persona but does not explain his choice of an Arab one. I suggest that Eliraz who, like many Israeli Jewish writers, politically identifies with left-wing ideology, chose Ibrahim as his alter ego to be able to express his own love for the sights and landscapes he had known as a child in pre-1948 Palestine and was now happy to see again. Since this was only made possible after the Israeli occupation of the West Bank in 1967, to which Eliraz personally objected, he chose to hide behind a West Bank Arab living away from his home town and to borrow his legitimate longing.

TRAVELLERS AS TRANSLATORS

Regarding travel writing as translation, Bassnett (1998c, 33) writes:

The enormous success of travel literature, particularly in the English speaking world, is increasingly the object of study. Post-colonial scholarship: has drawn attention to the implicit imperialist discourse in a great deal of travel literature, for travel writers create their portraits of other cultures explicitly for home consumption, thereby setting them up as the Other.

In terms of the axiom that sees translation as the product of its culture in dealing with other cultures and assuming that writings by travelers are translations (representations) of the cultures/societies they visit for their home/native audiences, such writings involve travelers approaching their material from a particular perspective, the perspective of the outsider: peeping through the lenses of their 'mother/native' culture with all its preexisting representations (master discourse) of the cultures being 'peeped at' by the travelers.

In travel writing, there is thus always an ideological dimension, albeit camouflaged as innocent accounts of journeys. Still, travel writing provides intriguing dimensions with regards to the considerable amount of translation inherent in them, including the use of strange linguistic forms like Pidgin English or Arabic dialects, for example.

A CASE OF PSEUDO-TRANSLATION

Given the above brief review of the issue of pseudo-translation (the term is used here in its very general sense), the remainder of this chapter examines the apparent auto-orientalism in *La Nuit sacrée* (as an instance of Arabic Literature in French, ALF for short and elsewhere), and its 'alien' translation into Arabic and how both texts may be no more than pseudo-translations of sorts. The discussion of both the 'assumed' French source text and its equally 'presumed' Arabic target text shows that both are examples of subverted representations of Morocco and by extension the Maghreb and the Arabs and Islam. Both serve to confirm Benjamin Barber's (1992) comments on the polarization of the modern world into western (civilized anti-terrorist) and the eastern (backward and terrorist—see chapter 1 in this volume).

Further and more importantly, both texts serve as instances of pseudo-translation: the French text invents source materials that do not at all reflect reality and the Arabic text serves no translationally intercultural encounters of any kind between the West (France) and the East (Maghreb and Islam).

ALF: PRELIMINARY REMARKS

The body of writings that has come to be known collectively as ALF is produced by writers who mostly originate from the Maghreb, particularly Morocco and Algeria, but also includes all Arab authors who use the French language in their writings.

For historical reasons, the Maghreb forms part of the Francophone world; a world into which French explorers and later colonialists brought their language and culture to 'civilize' the natives. Post-colonial ALF represents a unique instance: it is written in French yet about cultures and values that are not French but Arab, Berber and Islamic in spirit. Among its aims is the emphasis on the identification and exploration of the struggle to achieve national identity, and the valorization of ethnic, social, political, cultural and literary values.

ALF's main text is French, but it also draws on the languages of sub-texts, whether these be in standard Arabic, or Arabic as spoken in Maghrebi countries; or Berber and its varieties; as well as either mainstream Islamic culture or the various religious practices and sects that exist in the Maghreb. The position of this literature is important particularly that in the Maghreb books which are written in French, whether imported or locally produced, still represent close to 50 per cent of total book sales (Jaquemond, 1997).

The translation of ALF into Arabic, in itself quantitatively insignificant, does not simply refer to the conventional situation of translating across distant languages and cultures, but involves translating source texts which are themselves target texts—translations or rather pseudo-translations—back into target texts which are themselves source texts, the input for the technically French source texts. The issue, then, is not only turning texts written in the French language into Arabic, but the re-writing of texts, which are originally about the Maghreb.

Though most ALF can be seen as committed to challenging a dominant ideology, both external and internal, as well as the humanist and universal master discourse of the Gallic culture, some writers, notably Tahar Ben Jelloun, could be labelled as reinforcers of orientalist stereotypes and clichés about everything Arab and Islamic. They are native orientals or native foreigners, who contribute forcefully to a cultural dislocation through misrepresentation or pseudo-translation (akin to invented sources and travel logs as discussed above).

The growth of ALF and the existence of a considerable Maghrebi minority community in France have resulted in new challenges to, and redefinitions of, many notions of production and translation. Postcolonial ALF consists of texts with layerings of languages and cultures, which has resulted in a form of French with its own discursive strategies that defy the conventional definitions of source and target texts. Whilst the texts are generally written in standard French, they can rupture standard grammar and vocabulary through the infusion of indigenous vernaculars, customs and religious practices.

French discourses and discursive strategies are investigated from a somewhat privileged position: within (the French culture) and in-between two languages and two cultures (France and the Maghreb). In this context, Samia Mehrez (1992, 122) writes:

> the ultimate goal [of ALF] was to subvert hierarchies by bringing together the "dominant" and the "underdeveloped", by exploding and confounding different symbolic worlds and separate systems of signification in order to create a mutual interdependence and intersignification.

Within the framework of the relationships between the colonizer and the colonized, the aim of ALF and similar type of literature should be to bring to the fore the problematics of interculturation, bilingualism and identity. As a post-colonial enterprise, ALF should engage in readings, interpretations, and re-writings of spaces already occupied as well as the spaces of 'betweeness' that link France and French to the Maghreb with its languages, religion, ethnic diversity, pasts, presents and futures. Concerning this point, Larrivee (1994, 57) appropriately writes:

> Si le bilinguisme maghrébin contribue à iriscrire la littérature comme sujet de l'histoire, à son tour, l'écriture refait l'histoire, celle d'un sujet qui, paradoxalement s'efface en elle. En ce sens, on peut dire qu'il existe "des français", comme il existe des écrivains et des langues. La litterature maghrebine que l'on dit d'-expression française est en fait, selon Khatibi, "récit de traduction", traduction d'une langue familière autre, mais aussi traduction du français en français.

> If Maghrebi bilingualism contributes to the inscription of literature as a subject of history, writing, then, rewrites history, a history of a subject that, paradoxically, melts within it. In this sense, we can say that there are "French" as there are writers and languages. Maghrebi literature of French expression is in effect, according to Khatibi, a "narrative of translation": translation from a familiar, yet other, language, and translation from French into French. (my translation from French).

The majority of ALF writers have produced texts that aim to resist and liberate. Their writings show alternations of two discourses which reflect on one another in the interrogation, modification and/or negation of certain histories as well as the (re)construction of awarenesses of these histories. Their texts are generally closer to standard French, but include considerable references, including names, to Arabic, Berber and Islamic signs: all represented through alternative narrative techniques.

The problem for ALF texts, which are mainly published in France or under the auspices of French publishers outside France, is whether the dominant culture and its language will accept and interact equitably with the differences these texts present, or whether they will try and force them to assimilate into French value systems and its master discourse.

Whilst certain texts have received attention from French academic and journalistic critics, as well as the general readership, only a few writers maintain noticeable presence in the French literary and intellectual arenas. This is because, as Jacquemond (1997) appropriately argues, for ALF texts to achieve such noticeable presence, they need to conform to major criteria:

1) Dominant representations of Arab culture and society.
2) Dominant French ideological, moral, and aesthetic values.

Ben Jelloun seems to have opted to conform to both of these criteria/conditions. In *La Nuit sacrée,* for which he was awarded the prestigious prize, Prix Goncourt, in 1987 and which sold around two million copies, as well as in all his other writings, Ben Jelloun has inhabited the space of the *délire, fantasmes and fabulation.* These attributes perfectly realize the two major criteria/conditions for acceptance of the other (Ben Jelloun as the comer from the ex-colony) by the self (the French culture).

LA NUIT SACRÉE: THE ASSUMED FRENCH 'SOURCE' TEXT

La Nuit sacrée tells the story of a female given the Arabic name of Zahra after almost twenty years living as a boy with the name of Ahmed. Zahra-Ahmed, the child of a wealthy father in Morocco, is brought up as a boy to safeguard the honor and fortune of the father and to conform to the dominant patriarchal system. Ben Jelloun gives a number of accounts of fantasy, sex, irrationality and mental illness, the same accounts used in orientalist texts to describe the Arabs and Islam. Ben Jelloun produces an essentially Western text by building on certain concepts of Islamic mysticism, whilst ignoring their historical contexts.

In *La Nuit sacrée*, Ben Jelloun makes numerous references to Islam and to its Book. These include the questions of children to the blind teacher (the Consul):

Puisque l'islam est la meilleure des religions, pourquoi Dieu a attendu si longtemps pour la faire repandre?" (79)

Since Islam is the best religion, why did God wait so long before revealing it? (my translation)

There are also implications that Islam condones rape and torture, sorcery and charlatanism. The text is littered with images of the dead and ghosts, precisely what some orientalist discourses maintain in their depiction of the Arabs and Islam. On this cultural perspective, Sayyid (1997, 1) writes:

> Ghosts are the remains of the dead. They are echoes of former times and former lives: those who have died but still remain, hovering between erasure of the past and the indelibility of the present—creatures out of time. Muslims too, it seems, are often thought to be out of time: throwbacks to medieval civilizations who are caught in the grind and glow of 'our' modern culture. It is sometimes said that Muslims belong to cultures and societies that are moribund and have no vitality—no life of their own. Like ghosts they remain with us, haunting the present.

In *La Nuit sacrée*, Ben Jelloun is aware of the fact that he is invisible and subversive in his representations of Arabs and Islam. He is quoted by Samia Mehrez (1992) as having said in a French television talk-show that it would have been impossible for him to write in Arabic in the same way he wrote in French due to the sensitivities and the taboo nature of the topics. This, I suggest, is a rather extraordinary statement. Is Arabic, as a living language, unable to handle his topics? Is the average Moroccan reader, or the wider Arab audience, unable to cope with what he has to say?

In the text, there are tacit implications that Islam condones rape, torture as well as sorcery and charlatanism. To readers in the West, these implications can only strengthen prevalent and fossilized views about all that is Arab and Islamic; in other words, the master discourse.

> Au nom de Dieu le Clément et le Miséricordieux, que le salut et la bénédiction de Dieu soient sur le dernier des prophètes, notre maître Mohammed, sur sa famille et ses compagnons. Au nom de Dieu le Trè-Haut. Louanges à Dieu qui a fait que le plaisir immense pour l'homme réside en l'intériorité chaude de la femme. Louanges à Dieu qui mis sur mon chemin ce corps nubile qui avance sur la pointe extrême de mon désir. C'est le signe de sa bénédiction, de sa bonté et de sa miséricorde. Louanges à Dieu, louanges à toi ma sœur qui me précède pour que je sente ton parfum, pour que je devine tes hanches et tes seins, pour que je rêve de tes yeux et de ta chevelure. Ma sœur continue d'avancer jusqu'au buisson qui sera une demeure pour nos corps assoiffés. Ne te retourne pas. Je suis exposé à l'amour, avec toi ma sœur, mon inconnue, envoyée par le destin pour témoigner de la gloire de Dieu sur l'homme et la femme qui vont s'unir à la tombée de la nuit. Je loue Dieu. Je suis son esclave. Je suis ton esclave, ne t'arrête pas, le soleil descend lentement et avec lui mon orgueil tombe en miettes. Au nom de Dieu le Clément. . . (61)

Then, this seeker of divine assistance for sexual purposes touches Zahra's sensual parts, undoes her trousers with his teeth before penetrating her.

The mutilation of sex organs is also used by Ben Jelloun as a form of revenge carried out in the name of religion: Zahra's sisters circumcise her to revenge what she did as Ahmed before the father's death.

> nous avons découvert les vertus de notre religion bien-aimée. La justice est devenue notre passion. La vérité notre idéal et notre obsession. L'islam, notre guide. . . . A présent, au nom de Dieu le Clément et le Miséricordieux, le Juste et le Très-Puissant, nous ouvrons la petite mallette . . . (159)

In line with orientalist representations of the Arabs and Islam, Ben Jelloun describes the Moroccan society as being irrational, depraved (fallen), childlike, raging, dark, angry and different. Thus the existence of another that is rational, virtuous, mature and normal.

Knowing that sex and Arab women, mysticism and religion appeal to his French readers, Ben Jelloun sets out to depict Arab-Islamic societies as a contrast to Christendom, the West and modernity. Islam, on the other hand, is generally identified with negative and antithetical terms. Hiding behind mysticism and straddling two cultures, one of which is attached to specific and diverse locales and histories, Ben Jelloun, the alien but familiar writer from Morocco, addresses his text primarily to readers in France (recall Carbonell, 1996: 81).

Here are three examples about savage habits of eating, obsession with sex and the irrational behavior of a people in allowing a blind person to be their garden keeper.

> Je pris mon petit déjeuner ā côté d'un routier de la Chaouia qui mangea une tête de mouton cuite à la vapeur, but une théière entière de thé à la menthe et à la chiba, puis rota plusieurs fois en remerciant Dieu et Marrakech de lui avoir servi un si bon repas matinal. . ... Quand il vit une jeune fille passer devant nous sur une Mobylette, il se lissa la moustache avec l'air de dire qu'après un tel petit déjeuner une petite, vierge de préférence, porterait son bonheur à son comble. (12)

> Tout autour de ce dessin les innombrables noms donnés au sexe féminin: l'huis, la bénédiction, la fissure, la miséricorde, le mendiant, le logis, la tempête, la source, le four, le difficile, la tente, le chaud, la couple, la folie, l'exquis, la joie, la vallée, le rebelle. . .(77)

> Il y avait bien un aveugle, gardien à l'entrée du jardin andalou . (150)

As in most of his writings, Ben Jelloun includes in *La Nuit sacrée* significant translated and/or transliterated passages from Arabic with their cultural and historical specifics altered. The text is not just about Moroccans but also, by extension, about other Maghrebis, Arabs and Muslims living in France. These groups struggle to incorporate old and new allegiances into what essentially remain hyphenated identities – trans-lated—within a society that perceives itself as non-hyphenated.

Conscious not to antagonize his French readers, Ben Jelloun avoids any reference to contacts, particularly sexual, between French females and the deprived, savage Moroccans. Instead, we are told that the female tourist who has sexual encounters with a Moroccan truck driver is German. Here as well subversion is at work through the manipulation of historical relations between the French and the German peoples.

Though *La Nuit sacrée* has been described by some as the model of ALF, it was the Prix Goncourt that located it within world literature and hastened its translation into Arabic. Even its 'celebrated' bilingualism does not make it oppositional to the French cultural representations – master discourse—of the Arabs and Islam. After all:

> Modern world culture has no difficulty in accommodating unstable signs and domesticated exotica, so long as neither conflicts radically with systems of profit. (Asad, 1995: 331).

La Nuit sacrée satisfies the requirements, but not those of resister and/or liberator. It avoids the political upheaval, economic mismanagement and serious social problems that are common features in the region. It also avoids addressing the complexity of the male-female dynamics that cannot be furthered by narratives such as Ben Jelloun's. These issues can only be appropriately and effectively considered within the contexts of the correlations as well as the contradictions between religion, history, laws, social realities, traditional-modern family fabrics, modernist versus conservative discourses, aspirations and economic dilemmas.

The prize-winning text avoids all these issues, focusing instead on ghosts and saints, sex, rape and mutilation in the name of Allah, satisfying along the way desires of a West still interested in new translations of the *One Thousand and One Nights* than in the intricacies of contemporary Arab literature (recall Said, 1995).

Not surprisingly, Ben Jelloun proceeds in a predictable, even predetermined direction: alien cultures, indigenous practices—often fabricated and/or exaggerated—are recuperated through a process of familiarization and assimilation to existing norms of the French culture and its master discourse.

THE 'PRESUMED' ARABIC 'TARGET' TEXT

Laylatu l-Qadr, the Arabic translation of *La Nuit sacrée*, appeared in 1987, the same year the French text was published and the same year it was awarded the Prix Goncourt. The translation appeared in a series called *'awdatu n-naS* (Lit. the return of the text), a series that aims to translate bestselling ALF works into Arabic and whose main sponsor is Éditions du Seuil, the French publisher of *La Nuit sacrée.*

Translating texts like Ben Jelloun's back into Arabic does not seem to serve any return of any kind. It does not stimulate any cultural innovation or positively assess indigenous traditions and identities. Such translations are mainly addressed to an elite of bilinguals, not the wider Maghrebi constituencies of readers.

The Arabic translation follows the same manipulative strategies so as to camouflage Ben Jelloun's initial subversion. The language is highly formal, often archaic, and the use of Islamic references in ways that most certainly aim to pacify the 'small deplorable' Moroccan and Arab readers. Ben Jelloun's overt faithfulness to his audience in metropolitan Paris, his enthusiasm for the extremes of exotica and his ways of representing Moroccan locales as godforsaken places devastate any proper appreciation of his work in Arabic.

The problem, thus, of translating such a text does not simply concern linguistic codes but rather the translation inherent in the French text and all the subversion that went into its writing.

Perhaps an appropriate start would be the translation of the main title. In the French Text (FT henceforth), Ben Jelloun opts for *La Nuit sacrée* which, to his French readers, intertextualizes with *Mille et une nuits* (*One Thousand and One Nights*). This strategy keeps his choices and the narrative in line with the requirements of exoticization and naturalization. The title, *La Nuit sacrée* then changes in chapter 2 to *La Nuit du destin*, a choice approximately equivalent in signification to the main title of the FT.

In the Arabic Text (AT henceforth) the translator chooses *laylatu l-qadr* (the night of destiny, fate or preordination) to render both the main title and that of chapter 2. Regarding this translational choice, Mehrez (1992, 128) notes:

> This Arabic title is not a literal translation of the French words which remain alien to the cultural referent provided by the Arabic sign. The bilingual reader, however, is bound to make these necessary translations as soon as he or she begins to read the French text. If anything, therefore, the French title (of the original) fails to translate the Arabic subtext in which the entire work is grounded . . . . Consequently, the French title is decentered and deterritorialized by the Arabic sign which the bilingual reader is expected to read/translate into the French text.

Though I tend to agree with the intentions underscoring Mehrez's argument, I have nonetheless two misgivings. First, borrowing from the Qur'an, a highly sensitive text, to translate the main title of the FT and that of its chapter 2 seems to be a calculated ploy to put some distance between the AT and its receiving constituencies. Second, any translation is first and foremost intended for monolingual not bilingual readers.

Elsewhere, the translator uses *ar-rawD al-'aaTir* (fragrant or perfumed meadow or garden) to translate both the title of chapter 4 *Le jardin parfumé* as well as the structure *Le jardin exotique* in chapter 9. Though lexical equivalence does not obtain here, the choice, however, is another example of the appropriation of the language to manipulate readers. The two words *ar-rawD al-'aaTir* not only usually refer to paradise in Arab-Islamic culture but also appear as constituent elements in the titles of some medieval Arabic texts about sexuality and related topics: aphrodisiacs, genitalia, sex practices, etc. The translator seems to play on these intertextual referents; bewildering the AT audience along the way.

In rendering the title of chapter 14, *La comédie du bordel*, the translator—perhaps sensing the sensitivity of the word *bordel*—opts for an archaism that is not easily nor readily intelligible to most average Arab readers. The translator uses *kumiidyaa l-maakhuur* (the comedy of the house of prostitution, or the comedy of the whorehouse) whereby he transliterates *comédie* into Arabic but archaicises the translation of *bordel*. An appropriate rendering would have been *mahzalat l-bordeiil* (the farce/comedy of the brothel) where the French word *bordel* is transliterated since it is already in common usage among the constituents of the target audience.

The AT overflows with uncommon and strange linguistic forms that reveal the translator's hand: a systematic use of archaisms on the lexical level which points to the desire to elevate the tenor to a formality that makes the language lofty and highbrow. The lexis is also characterized by numerous terms from specialized jargons: body parts and diseases.

The choices aim at increasing the conceptual density of the language and, thus, move it away from everyday language of the Moroccan society, in particular, and the wider Arab readership, at large. By their difficulty, such choices attract attention from and disturb the effects of the language that surrounds them. Lexical choices in the AT are in contrast with the unidiomatic lexis and style of the FT. Here are some representative examples.

> In the FT, what is common usage in French—*sans rien dire, sans rien repondre, je ne dis rien*—becomes in the AT *lam yanbus bibinti shafa* (Lit. not utter/speak/say the daughter of a lip). This is an archaic collocation that requires extra processing efforts to decipher unless of course the reader is bilingual. The translator could have opted for what, like the French structures, is common usage in Modern Arabic: *sakata* (kept silent) or *lam yaqul shay'an* (did not say anything). Here are some more examples of the same.

J'ai pleuré (34) becomes *inkharTtu fi l-bukaa'* (26) (Lit. I entered into/associated myself with crying] in lieu of bakaytu (I cried).

raméne (43) becomes *ya'uub* (34) (Lit. to come back with] instead of a word like *jalaba* (brought back).

filiformes (65) becomes *khayTiyyataa sh-shakl* (50) (Lit. filamentous] instead of something like, *naHifataan* or *naHiilataan* (Lit. skinny/thin).

eau pure (93) becomes *maa' namiir* (70) (good/pure/clear water) instead of *maa' Saafii* (pure water) for example.

les fesses (90) becomes ilyatayhaa (68) (her two buttocks), a technical term, instead of mu'akhiratuhaa (her backside) which is more colloquial and would, thus, be more intelligible.

Il me fallait pas (184) becomes kaana laa manduHata (145) (Lit. there was no alternative/choice/option for me) instead of the common usage kaana 'alayya (I had to).

What shows an underlying consciousness on the part of the translator to choose such strange structures and lexicon is the fact that for the examples cited above, and many more in the AT, vowels are provided to assist at least pronunciation when vowels are not usually provided in Arabic texts.

The AT also contains a number of adaptations of French words through transliteration: *smoking* (11/9), *naphtaline* (124/97), *babouches* (187/148). There is also the use of technical terms for diseases and different body parts that accompany rape and sex—usually lengthy passages. Consider: *al-'uDwu l-jinsii l-'unthawii* (the female sexual organ) instead of what is common like *farj* (vagina). Such lexis could easily occur in a Friday sermon at a mosque and certainly in technical dictionaries and medical textbooks. The most telling example, perhaps, is the translation of *bougainvillées* (35) into Arabic as *jahanamiyyaat* (26). Realizing the strangeness of such a term, the translator provides a footnote. The irony, however, is that the footnote itself turns out to be too technical and in need of a footnote itself. All this puts added information-processing burdens on the reader.

One might argue that perhaps the translator's aim is to address a wider pan-Arab audience and not just the Moroccan or the Maghrebi ones. But, the fact that the translator uses a typically Moroccan Arabic lexis to describe all that is Moroccan: tea and its ingredients, *biit l-ma* (Lit. the room of water [i.e., toilet]), food, clothes, words that denote streets, alleyways (*derb, zanqa*), certain narcotics (*kif*) would all make intelligibility for Arabs from the Middle East, for example, extremely demanding if not impossible. I should note here that the words related to specifically Moroccan items are merely transliterated from the French for Ben Jelloun uses them transliterated in his FT, for a purpose, of course.

Aware of the sensitivity of handling passages from the Qur'an and of the pride the Arabs have in their poetry, Mohammed Sharghi, the translator, intervenes in the presentation of Qur'anic and poetry quotations, which are given in large, bold fonts, and appropriately introduced. So, *Dieu a dit* (God said) becomes *fii qawlihi tacaalaa* (in His [exalted/raised far above] words) where the tense, past in the FT, is not marked at all. The French *quatre phrases* (four sentences), which introduces an excerpt from Arabic poetry, becomes *baytayn* (two verses or two lines), echoing the structure of the Arabic classical *Qasiida*, the canonized genre of Arabic classical poetry, ode. What is more peculiar is that the Arabic translation of the poetry is not equivalent to the FT. An excerpt from page 41 of the FT runs as follows:

> Nous sommes les enfants, les hôtes de la terre.
> Nous sommes faits de terre et nous lui reviendrons.
> Pour nous, terrestres, le bonheur ne dure guère,
> mais des nuits de bonheur effacent l'affiiction.

> We are the children, the guests of earth.
> We are made of earth, and return to it we shall.
> For us, terrestrials, happiness barely lasts,
> but nights of happiness remove the infliction.
> (my translation)

For which the Arabic translation gives the following:

> wa lammaa 'an tajahhamanii muraadii
> jaraytu ma'a zzamaani kamaa 'araadaa

> wa hawwantu l-khaTuuba 'alyya Hattaa
> ka 'annii Sirtu 'amnaHuhaa l-widaadaa

> And, when my aim got sick of me,
> I ran the way time ran

> And, I lessened the effects of my misfortunes until I felt as if offering them affection.
> (my translation)

It would appear that the translator may have taken the liberty to quote other parts of the poem, which he felt would be more effective. The translator's aim could be to modify the cognitive environment of the receivers of the AT, and achieve particular illocutionary effects.

Through a combination of archaisms, unusual syntax and punctuation, concretization and adaptations, the AT manages to portray the blurred relationship between reality and fantasy, strange events and characters that Ben Jelloun employs, perhaps, to camouflage his exoticization.

One final point worthy of note is that the translator also retains all intertextual references, as well as references to French literary figures, without offering any assistance which would allow the reader to locate them. For instance *Ulysses* and *Hamlet* are simply transliterated as *'uliis* and *hamlit* respectively. The contributions of these intertextualities are not easily retrievable in the AT.

CONCLUDING REMARKS

Given its special status, the resistant dimension of ALF is matched only by the subverted representations of the Maghreb by some post-French colonialism writers. This is because it is these writers who ought to unravel narratives and give the oppressed from the Maghreb, and the wider Arab World, a voice in history through the provision of critical interrogations of the master discourse that reports native realities by both mainstream Western writers and the elites left behind by the old colonial order. This is particularly true for writers from the Maghreb because, unlike British colonialism, the French emphasized assimilation among indigenous elites and worked to repress the writing and teaching of Maghrebi languages and cultures.

Instead of presenting an exploration of the relationships between opposites: racial, religious, social, linguistic or a critique of 1980s society in Morocco, Ben Jelloun's *La Nuit sacrée* and its equally alien translation into Arabic merely affirm their status as Western texts, but written by non-Westerners: orientals, native foreigners. Emanating from the other, this is a gratifying situation.

The following quote from Wole Soyinka (1976, x) appropriately describes where Ben Jelloun and his text as well as the Arabic 'pseudo-translation' into Arabic can be located.

We . . . have been blandly invited to submit ourselves to a second epoch of colonialism—this time by a universal-humanoid abstraction defined and conducted by individuals whose theories and prescriptions are derived from the apprehension of their world and their history, their social neuroses and their value system.

Though quantitatively insignificant, the translation of ALF into Arabic does not involve the conventional translational situation of two distant languages and cultures. Rather, it involves texts which are themselves target

texts in French – translations of some kind. The problem with translations like
the AT is not only turning texts written in French into Arabic but the rewriting of texts about something originally Maghrebi; almost self-translation
whereby a culture translates texts *about it back for it*. Furthermore, wasting
time and resources on such translations neither serves the Moroccan society
nor the cause of translation into Arabic.

Discussing the similar case of Indians writing in English, Dyson (1993,
178-9), distinguishes between bilingual creativity and monolingual creativity
however many languages such writers master. Regarding the case of Salman
Rushdie, a writer not dissimilar from our Ben Jelloun, Dyson (quoted in
Prasad, 1999: 46) writes:

> Salman Rushdie interlards his English with Urdu words and phrases as a
> naughty teenager interweaves his speech with swearwords, but he cannot write
> a book in Urdu . . . He may be a cosmopolitan, but he is a monolingual writer.
> His use of Urdu adds colour to his texts, but does not lead us to an Indian intel-
> lectual world. Had he been an artist in Urdu, I doubt if he would have used the
> language to pepper his English in the facetious way he does now.

To bring this chapter to a close, I cite the following quote from Jacquemond (1997, 157) that is absolutely relevant and applicable to *La Nuit sacrée*;
a work that leans itself heavily on translation, and throws light on *Laylatu l-
Qadr*, its arabically alien translation:

> Et ces "documents" sont d'autant mieux reçus qu'ils viennent confirmer à la fois
> l'altérité de l'autre culture (arriérée, autoritaire . . .) et la représentation que la cul-
> ture française se donne d'elle même (moderne, démocratique . . .)—confirmation
> qui, venant de l'autre, n'est que plus gratifiante.

> Such documents are well received because they simultaneously confirm the al-
> terity of the other culture (backward, authoritarian . . .), and the representation the
> French culture bestows upon itself (modern, democratic ..); *a confirmation, em-
> anating from the other, is utterly gratifying*. (emphasis added; my translation).

Chapter Four

A Case of Self-translation

When an author is his or her own translator, he or she creates a situation which in turn generates a number of valid questions:

1. What leads someone to decide to translate their own work in the first place?
2. How do authors-cum-translators approach the source text (their own), and the translation process?
3. What happens to the issues of position, power, visibility, fidelity, etc. in translations produced by authors of the source text?
4. How, more importantly, does the author-cum-translator perceive the target readership, particularly if the latter shares the same native language and culture as the author turned translator?
5. What, equally importantly, happens to the semiotic status of the original through translation by its author?

These are the questions this chapter aims to address. The discussion of the infrequent situation of author-cum-translator (either as individuals or cultures) focuses on two instances that represent both cases: *Autumn of Fury* (1983) written in English by Heikal (an Arab writer and intellectual) and the Arabic translation (1988) produced by Heikal himself (as instance one), and the translation of the Islamist text *Milestones* (1981), written in Arabic by Qutb, into English by seemingly Muslim translators (1990).

SELF-TRANSLATION

A valid general perception is that authors and translators complement each other. But translators are frequently criticised for betraying authors through inaccurate, inappropriate and at times manipulatory translations. The grounds for such criticism vary from the purely linguistic to the more functional, cultural and beyond. However, it remains that humanity needs both authors and translators.

This situation exists because few translators have been 'great' authors in their own right, although most, if not all, cultures offer examples of authors who are also translators. The contributions of these authors as translators are usually well received since, on the one hand, translating is not their main job, and on the other, they are authors and are thus assumed to show more sense of and sensibility for the works they translate – their own works.

It is however safe to say that by and large translators have not been authors themselves. Those authors who sometimes assume the role of translator do so as an incidental way of further developing their own talents or as a tribute to other authors they admire. Block (1981), for example, discusses three French authors turned translators (Nerval, Baudelaire, and Gide) and concludes by arguing that the case of these three French authors suggests that,

> the translator has need of the same imaginative qualities as the novelist, playwright, or poet, and that great translations require the simultaneous presence of unusual linguistic and literary talents in a single person. Translation in the hands of gifted writers is not reproduction but creation, fully deserving of the same informed critical response as other modes of literary endeavor. (124-5)

It is equally true that authors rarely translate their own works; the task being left to translators. Whereas in the past translations of great works often took lengthy periods of time, now, with the globalization of human culture and the desire of publishers for quick returns, most bestsellers are often hastily translated. Many authors consequently find themselves filing legal cases to prevent further publication of thrown-together translations of their works. Kuhiwczak (1990) gives the example of Milan Kundera, the East European novelist, who has spent more time fighting and correcting inappropriate and often misleading translations of his novels in the West than channelling his energy into creating more novels.

INSTANCE ONE: THE MANIPULATING AUTHOR-CUM-TRANSLATOR

Written in English, *Autumn of Fury* gives an exciting account of the life of the late Egyptian president Anwar Sadat who was assassinated in October 1981 by members of his own army. The focus of the book is on Sadat's policies which, according to the author, have had disastrous ramifications for Egypt and the rest of the Arab World. I should note here that Heikal was imprisoned, along with a large number of others, by Sadat and was released after the assassination.

The front cover of the English text (ET) shows the main title *Autumn of Fury* followed by the subtitle *The Assassination of Sadat*. Though Heikal keeps the main title of his book intact on the front cover of the Arabic Text (AT), the subtitle, however, changes into *The story of the beginning and end of Anwar Sadat's era* * (* indicates my back translation from Arabic).

The subtitle on the front cover of the AT is the first indication of Heikal's intentions to manipulate and appropriate Arab readers' reactions and the ways he wants them to interpret and read his text. His manipulation of the subtitle is a case of the highest levels of invisibility or what one can call 'visible invisibility'. On the one hand, the front cover of the AT does not mention at all that it is a translation, but gives the impression that it was originally written in Arabic. On the other hand, Heikal's appropriation reflects his attempt at using what is semiotically familiar, thus unchallenging, to Arab readers.

The words he uses—*story, beginning and end* and *era**—all form part of the way Arabs generally perceive history and progress and hit at the very heart of their religious belief system which, compared with European equivalents, has a strong influence and effect on their view of life and death. In other words, it is easy for an Arab reader to accept the ideas of beginning and end of an era as being part of and attributable to the divine will.

The word *assassination* would have not triggered the same reaction in the readers of the AT. But to an English language reader, *assassination* sums up that mysterious, violent, fundamentalist, autocratic, but also exotic Arab World. Here, and like those Western translators to whom Venuti (1995; 1998), Carbonell (1996) and Kuhiwczak (1990) respectively refer to as invisible, subverters, and appropriationists, Heikal gives Western readers what is familiar to them: an Arab World where peace-makers are assassinated.

Now onto the introduction. Like any written within an English tradition, the introduction of the ET runs to five pages setting the scene for the book and ending with the author acknowledging his debt to all those who helped him in any way, and reiterating the familiar statement that he alone assumes responsibility for any errors of fact or judgement.

The translation of this introduction in the AT runs more or less in the same way as that of the ET until the last paragraph. All the Arab academics mentioned in the ET appear in the AT but one sentence is omitted:

> Finally, I would again wish to thank my friend and colleague, Edward Hodgkin, for all the assistance he has given me in writing this book (p. 7).

Here Heikal aware of the sensitivity of the issue, eliminates any reference to a non-Arab who assisted him because otherwise Arab readers may interpret the writing of the ET in the first place as some kind of a conspiracy designed to vilify the Arab World. They may conclude that Heikal is nothing less than an agent for the 'external enemies' of Egypt and the Arab World. Heikal adds to the introduction in the AT the following statement:

> And, I have tried to be no more than a witness of an important and strange period in Egypt's history (p. 22).*

This statement is intended to direct readers of the AT who culturally believe that messengers are not to be harmed in any way regardless of the news they bring. By positioning himself as a witness, Heikal deliberately distances himself from the judgements he makes about Sadat and his presidency and tries to make Arab readers believe that he is a mere 'objective' reporter of events.

The translation of the introduction in the AT is preceded by two introductions: one for Egyptian readers and one for the wider Arab readership. The two introductions, not found in the ET, go into details about the reasons why the book should be read in a particular way, i.e., that it simply chronicles (Heikal = chronicler) events that led to what happened on October 6th, 1981 (the assassination of Sadat) and not as an account of Heikal's own assessment of Sadat's rule. But, it is a truism to say that language is both itself and its circumstances, and that any text is bound to represent in varying degrees its socio-cultural context and the position of its author.

The two introductions in the AT run to 10 pages of explanations and instructions on how to approach the text. One of the reasons given by Heikal for deciding to undertake himself the translation of something written in English about something Arab back into Arabic, is that the level of debate the book generated has been such that he could not let other translators do the job for this highly sensitive book. But even here Heikal manipulates the Arab readership by indicating that the outcry the ET created may be due to the fact that

> a lot of people benefited during Sadat's rule, and consequently do not wish to see his legacy tarnished because they will ultimately lose all that they had previously amassed (AT: 14).*

This camouflaged reference to political and ultimately financial corruption in the Arab World is cleverly intended by Heikal to turn all potential enemies into allies. Appealing further to Arab readers, and ultimately hoping to shape their reading of the AT, Heikal labels Sadat's reign in Egypt *an historical mistake,* which he maintains is worse than any other crimes. This, it seems to me, is intended to play on the feelings of most Arabs, who viewed Sadat as someone who weakened the Arab nation by going it alone and signing the Camp David peace treaty with Israel in 1979.

At the end of the AT, Heikal includes two letters which do not appear in the ET. The first letter, one page and a half long, was written by Al-Hakim, an Egyptian writer, comparing Heikal's *Autumn of Fury* with a book he wrote himself about Nasser's rule. Al-Hakim wrote his book in Arabic, however. In his lengthy response to this letter, in over eight pages, Heikal expresses his dismay at all those Arabs who did not read the book, yet passed judgements and conclusions. But what is extremely interesting in Heikal's letter is that he states that his book

> Autumn of Fury, was not meant for the Arab World, otherwise he would have written it in Arabic (p. 473).*

Accordingly, the book was aimed at the outside English language reading world, the other, and not the Arabic language reading world: us/we, the author's own people and culture.

The back cover of the ET lists excerpts from reviews:

- Compulsively readable,
- a formidable indictment of the Sadat's years,
- a riveting account,
- a brilliant sense of history, devastating . . . eloquent power.

These sentences clearly indicate that the book was generously received by the English language reading world, because it stays within the familiar (master discourse) and yet at the same time foreign parameters, and because Heikal successfully manipulated the English language readers by telling them what they are used to being told about the mysterious, violent and president-assassinating world.

The back cover of the AT, however, carries a paragraph written by none other than Heikal himself. The paragraph further tells the Arab readers that they should remember

> the text as a mere account of the reasons that led to the assassination of Sadat and as an attempt to explain why Sadat's end came the way it did.*

Another of Heikal's manipulatory ploys involves his use of photographs. In the ET, 16 different photographs of Sadat are stacked between pages 156 and 157. They are not numbered and can be taken out without affecting the overall flow of the text. In the AT, however, 33 photographs of Sadat are strategically spread throughout the text in a way that makes them form a sub-text without which the text itself will lose its structural design and its information flow.

In the case of *Autumn of Fury*, the author finds himself in a complex position. He tries to manipulate the position which readers of the translation are assumed to occupy. He does so by blurring his reading position as a translator and his position as the author of the original, while all the time laying claim to objectivity in his translation. Objectivity (vs. subjectivity) is a subtle way of positioning oneself along the authorship-readership continuum.

Heikal subjectively manipulates Arab readers to position themselves where he wants them, not where their status as readers would normally allow them. He blurs the distances between author, reader and translator, with the ultimate goal of steering Arab readers into a particular position and consequently a particular reading mode that makes their own interpretations of the text almost impossible (Faiq, 2001).

The problem for Heikal is that what he made familiar and natural for the English language reading world, and which, according to him, was not meant for Arab readers, wants to be born again Arab. But this is not an easy task. How can one refamiliarize and renaturalize something Arab that was forcibly shaped for a particular non-Arab audience? Heikal's cunning strategy was to turn invisibility, subversion and appropriation around. This he did through a sustained and systematic manipulation of the reading position and ultimately of the readers. He generally succeeds in renativizing what he denativized utilizing all powers available to him as the author (owner) of the English source text and as the translator/author (owner) of the Arabic target text. But in the process, he made Arab readers look like 'deplorable small peoples,' to use Kuhiwczak's (1990) words.

INSTANCE TWO: WHEN A CULTURE SELF-TRANSLATES

While instance one of self-translation discussed above deals with an Arab writer writing in English about his culture then deciding to carry out the translation of the same text into Arabic, instance two here deals with a wider perspective of self-translation: When a culture decides to carry out the translation of its own texts into target languages for target cultures.

The instance discussed here relies on an article by Holt (2004) on the translation of an iconic Islamic (Islamist in today's terminology depending on the user's perspective) text, *Milestones,* written in Arabic by Sayyid Qutb (a leader of the Muslim Brotherhood in Egypt) and translated by an Islamic publishing house without any reference to the identity of the actual translators.

Basing his discussion on the rise and characteristics of what is nowadays labelled Islamist discourse and which is becoming increasingly important in political and cultural life in the Arab World and world-wide, Holt (2004, 63) appropriately posits that the

> translation of this discourse is . . . of particular interest, not only because of its prevalence and importance but because of the particular problems it poses theoretically and practically.

On the basis of the discussion in chapters 1 and 2 in this volume, Islamist discourse (as a discourse competing with and challenging the master discourses of both its own native cultures and societies and that of the West, particularly American discourse on terrorism and *jihadism*) speaks from outside the orbit of its cultures and the West to challenge notions of universality based on European models. Yet few have made any serious attempts to explore the basic and fundamental tenants as well as the textual practices of this discourse.

The cultural encounters that precede any translation act influence intercultural communication when a discourse like Islamist discourse is translated. Holt (2004, 63) writes:

> Some writers . . . [like Sayyid Qutb] have been hugely influential in the Arab world but are rarely read by Western readers. More often than not, they read second-hand accounts filtered and digested for them by Western based academics, always open to the charge of orientalism. So, all the more reason for Islamists to be heard directly or as directly as translation allows and all the more reason why the translators' art must be closely scrutinised. We need to see if a text expressly antithetical to another culture can be translated into the language of that 'Other.'

Even at the lexical level and given the discussion in chapter 1 of this volume, terms that are central in Islamist discourse such as *Jihad* come with layerings of connotative meanings. The travelling of such terms across the space between (and betwixt) its domain of signification to be recuperated by readers of a very different discourse whose domain comes ingrained with chains of meanings about the culture of the source discourse, makes the potential for 'slippage' very strong, hence misunderstanding, misrepresentation and even cultural confrontation.

Part of the Western cultures' apparent lack of knowledge or preparedness to know about Islamist discourse is in opposition to the situation on the other side of the cultural spectrum. In his book, Qutb acknowledges the 'existence' of the West, its culture and material progress, but naturally and expectedly he chose to 'root the whole debate in terms related to Muslim theology and history', and frequently refers to 'the multi-ethnicity of companions of the Prophet of Islam and to the fact that Islam does not distinguish between believers on the basis of race or nationality' (*op. cit.*, 67) as evidence of equality and the respect of human rights within Islam, and that his book seeks 'praxis, not abstract theorising.'

The case of translating such a sensitive text demonstrates how, in the age of globalisation, discourses that find themselves on the margins of the periphery of the centre of this globalisation and its master discourse, attempt to establish themselves by forcing their own master discourse and rupturing the target language along the way, forcing the target reader to do the travelling across the cultural space all the way to where the source text resides.

So, the members of source text culture (perhaps converted Westerners to Islam in the case discussed here) decide to take it upon themselves to carry out the translation act. In such cases, the conventional directionality of translation is turned around, whereby the target readers are made to travel to the source text, producing thus a wholly foreignised translation product. The following examples taken from Holt (2004) represent some of the strategies adopted by the translators of Qutb's book.

A perusal of the target text shows that the translation has retained a great deal of *Arabicness*. Holt (2004) lists four major examples of such Arabicness from what may be familiar to the alien as far as the target readership is considered.

- Arabic words that are now almost assimilated into English, such as *Islam*, *Muslim*, *Allah*, the *Qur'an*, and others may serve a stronger cultural force if kept in transliteration (phonemic translation) as their force and chains of articulation remain unaffected, although not in the same manner as those achieved on the Arabic language reader.
- Quotations from the Qur'an and *Hadith* (traditions of the Prophet of Islam) translated into English cause this language readership 'confusion' because of the inconsistencies in references and footnotes.
- Arabic expressions and structures that are central in Islam are almost all given in transliterations with some glosses in English pose virtually no problems for Arabists and those conversant with Islam, but cause reception problems that seriously affect readability for the average English language reader.
- Arabic terms that covey key concepts in Islam are likewise merely transliterated. Such terms include *jahiliyya* and *din* (pre-Islam period and religion respectively).

These instances of specific translational choices indicate that the translator(s) seem(s) to have decided that the 'stability and the specificity' of Islamic terminology are too important and sensitive to render them into English through terminology that has different chains of meanings and referents. Using equivalent terms in English may ultimately lead to the fracturing of the cohesion and coherence of the master discourse of Islam. For the translator(s), the intention may have been not to allow the English language reader to project onto the text meanings and significations that exist in their own master discourse (Islam).

> Like the source text, the translation appears to have been written for a vanguard, for a readership already conversant not only with intertextual reference but with the surface forms of Qur'anic Arabic . . . In short, this version cannot be read by a monolingual, monocultural English reader. . . . There is a certain logic to a book originally written for Muslim activists in Egypt to be translated for a corresponding readership in English but it is unfortunate that such an influential work cannot reach a wider audience, particularly given the widespread misconceptions about Islam and the Arab world that are prevalent in the West. For an English translation to reach such a wider audience, a new version would have to be commissioned, one which relies less on transliteration and which makes intertextual references more manifest.
> (Holt 2004, 73-4)

BY WAY OF CONCLUDING

Within the semiotics of communication, the status of something being a text is conditioned by the shared and/or assumed knowledge that the author(s) and the reader(s) each position(s) himself/herself, through a process of projecting onto the text their absent counterpart(s). Both author and reader can only occupy one position vis-à-vis a particular text. When we talk of translation, the same positions do not change dramatically. A translator assumes the role of a reader first and then endeavours to mirror the position of the author through translation.

In the case of our instance one, the English text itself represents an instance of translation giving the English language readers what they are generally familiar with as represented and stereotyped through the politics and ideologies of the power dictated by the other and through the master discourse these readers' culture (with invisibility, subversion, or appropriation—see chapters 1 and 2 in this volume).

In this respect, the figure of the author and/or translator appears as authority to the unknown: Arab politics and culture: an exotic, yet violent East. Heikal's Arabic translation of his own English text, belittlingly tells readers how to make meaning out of words. But, the question remains whether an author-cum-translator can assume the right to be more subversive, more invisible, more appropriationist and more manipulative, while we would cry foul were he or she an 'ordinary' translator?

The English translation of an important text of Islamist discourse by apparently Muslim translators (members of the culture of the source text) raises interesting issues not only for intercultural and translation studies, but also for international relations. A discourse that has been manipulated and misrepresented for centuries writes back and controls its representations (translations) for members of other cultures, particularly the hegemonic one (the culture of the English language). The strategy used is one that forces the target reader to travel to the source text through a sustained foreignization strategy.

The two instances of self-translation discussed here are by no means rare. They happen constantly, consciously or subconsciously. Because translation, with its master discourse, regulates differences, it and the differences become problematic in the exchange of cultural goods, particularly what concerns identity and power relations.

Chapter Five

A Case of Translation Historiography

Today, translation stands as a fundamental principle describing almost anything that relates to interaction between languages, cultures, subjects, or objects. This characterization of what translation and translating are and what they involve demonstrates how the field of translation studies has come a long way.

Culture in and of translation has been given prominence in considering the traffic of texts across boundaries and a focus on what happens in and during the negotiation of the space in-between sources and targets has led to the examination of far-reaching ramifications of translation, which has, for decades, been seen mostly as a 'simplex' process of transfer across languages.

This paradigm shift in the meaning translation has, also highlights the necessity of considering the historical development of cultures and how each has associated a particular politics (master discourse) for translation as it deals with the 'mess' created by the 'Babelesque confusion.'

Different cultures have, at different times in their histories, developed and/or adapted to or adopted techniques and strategies, discourses of translation, and considered them synonymous with translation and with translating others.

It is within this context that an examination of the history of translation is vital for a discipline that affects the contact between peoples interculturally (even intraculturally). However, the young discipline of translation studies requires not history as a narrative of events of the past(s), rather it requires historiography, which refers to a particular discourse about historical events that is organized and analyzed along specific non-mainstream historical principles.

Translation was the first and basic means for civilized interaction (from hieroglyphy into Greek, from Greek into Syriac, from both into Arabic, and finally from Arabic into Latin and other European languages, and today from the latter to the rest of the World), a historiography of translation should examine translation as a cultural movement that stems from and affects crisis, nation-building and identity.

Interlingual traffic between different peoples and civilizations through translation has been a vital means in the evolution, strengthening and even the creation of national literary and cultural identities. Developments in the study of what translation involves and what ramifications it has have widened to cover issues almost unrelated to what seems to be an 'obvious' activity. In this context, Bassnett & Trivedi (1999, 2) succinctly write:

> [T]ranslation does not happen in a vacuum, but in a continuum; it is not an isolated act, it is part of an ongoing process of intercultural transfer. Moreover, translation is a highly manipulative activity that involves all kinds of stages in the process of transfer across linguistic and cultural boundaries. Translation is not an innocent, transparent activity but is highly charged with signification at every stage; it rarely, if ever, involves a relationship of equality between texts, authors or systems.

Because it brings language and culture together, translation is thus by its very nature a multi-problematic process with different manifestations and realizations in various cultures/traditions (see chapter 2 in this volume for a discussion of the master discourse of translation).

In assessing the function of translation as process and product, I posit that the concepts of 'monitoring' and 'managing,' as explained by Beaugrande and Dressler (1981), would be useful tools for positioning a particular translation project in history according to a historiographical perspective. Monitoring refers to the expounding of texts without intervention while managing involves steering texts towards specific goals and intentions.

The aim of this chapter is to assess what history labels Medieval Arabic Translation (MAT, for short and henceforth) in terms of its culture and in terms of how it dealt with accommodating foreign cultures into Arabic, a hitherto predominantly literary language and of limited geopolitical influence.

MAT: A HISTORICAL SYNOPSIS

Shortly after the establishment of the Islamic polity in the seventh century A.D., the Arabs (Muslims) recognised the importance of translation for spreading their new faith and strengthening their new state, *Ummah*. The

Arabs were among the first in history to establish translation as a government enterprise. Successive rulers made it part of the government with its own budget and institutions.

MAT gained momentum early in the eighth century A.D. when Arabs started to produce paper on a large scale, and reached its zenith in the ninth and tenth centuries. In its historical development, MAT moved from a necessity phase through a truly golden and glorious phase to a phase of decline. In general terms, three main features characterized MAT.

1. Diversity of sources: Arabs translated from any language they came in contact with in the course of their conquests: Hindi, Persian, Syriac, and Sanskrit. Their main source language, however, was Greek.
2. Extensiveness: MAT, particularly in Baghdad in the east and Cordoba in the west, covered almost all areas of knowledge of the time, including mathematics, astronomy, philosophy, logic, medicine, chemistry, engineering, politics, and geography.
3. Organization: In the eighth century, translation was seen as a necessity with the focus on medicine and warfare. In the ninth and tenth centuries, translation was made an official undertaking. The rulers encouraged translators, and even enticed them to translate by giving them—so the anecdote goes—the equivalent weight of translations in gold. The Abbasid Caliph al-Ma'moun (reign 813-833) also established the *house of wisdom* (*baytu l-Hikma*), which was the equivalent of a modern centre of excellence or academy. The main political and cultural concern of the rulers was to make Arabic the language of knowledge and learning, not only the language of poetry and religion. In this they succeeded, as Arabic remained the main international donor language for centuries.

The Caliph al-Ma'moun is historically seen as the champion of MAT. He recruited translators including non-Muslims from different parts of the world as long as they met the strict criteria to function as translators. He made translators state employees with regular incomes. He also organized *baytu l-Hikma* into departments for translation, editing, research, publication and general scholarship.

According to Khouri, in one of his peace treaties with Byzantium, al-Ma'moun demanded as reparation a whole library in Constantinople. Nutting (1964, 125) sums up the cultural and intellectual aspects of al-Ma'moun's reign:

With a deep love of the arts and sciences, he [al-Mamoun] became the greatest of all caliphal patrons of poetry, theology, philosophy, astrology and astronomy.

He encouraged and imported men of learning regardless of race or religion. Christians, Greeks, Jews, Zoroastrians—even heathen Sabians whose star-worshipping was thought to make them experts in astronomy—were patronized and pampered in order that they might enrich the caliphate with their knowledge and creative power. The stream of culture that had earlier flowed into Greece from its sources in Egypt, Babylonia, Phoenicia and Judaea now poured back to refertilize the areas of its origins.

Al-Ma'moun also encouraged publication by Arab scholars and insisted that translation was only a first step in surpassing former civilizations and in creating a distinct national Arab/Islamic identity.

With the Arab-Islamic state firmly established and its resources diversified, the political decision was made that, to keep the state strong, it needed science and technology. This triggered the sustained and large-scale translation of major books in various fields of learning.

From glory, MAT moved to a phase of chaos and decline, which can be attributed to two main factors:

1. The debate between different Islamic schools and between Muslims and other religious groups about Islam and interpretations of its book, the Qur'an, made Muslims decide that they needed philosophy—in particular logic—in order to debate argue their particular philosophy or interpretation of religion and other topics.
2. Translation became fashionable. In addition to the state, rich families and individuals sponsored translation projects, established private translation bureaux and commissioned translations, often given as gifts to rulers (Faiq, 2006b). Notwithstanding its contribution to MAT, private sponsorship was also responsible for ushering in the chaotic phase. This period also coincided with internal political divisions in the Arab-Islamic empire and with the demise of strong central government. Translation lost its national momentum and became attached to individuals' and patrons' tastes, rather than national planning and aspirations.

Like all translators through history, medieval Arab translators faced immense problems in rendering foreign works into Arabic, which, until the rise of Islam, was a mainly literary language. They had to assimilate new subjects and find appropriate equivalents for alien concepts in Arabic. The main problems they faced were terminological and, accordingly, most early translations remained inscrutably foreign and were revised, amended and at times even recarried out. These translators adopted three main strategies: literal, semantic and gist.

1. In literal translation, the translators considered each source language word and its meaning and then used Arabic approximations. This often meant that they transliterated technical terms that produced stilted and odd structures and style in the Arabic rendition. This strategy was predominant during the early or necessity phase of MAT.
2. Translators of the golden age adopted the semantic strategy which involved reading the original, processing it and trying to find semantically equivalent structures in Arabic regardless of lexical equivalence. Most translations produced according to this strategy did not require any revision or rewriting.
3. Later translators adopted gist translation, a strategy that involved summaries rather than full translations. This strategy came into use when the need for translation from Greek and other languages diminished as Arab scholars started to produce their own research. Gist translation was also characteristic of a new breed of translators who were competent in both the languages and the subjects with which they dealt.

There were strict criteria for recruiting translators, particularly during the glorious phase of MAT. As quoted in Khouri (1988, 54), al-Jahid, a medieval Arab scholar and critic who stressed the relativity of translation, particularly poetic translation, stipulated the following main criteria for translators:

- a full understanding of the subject matter,
- an awareness of current methods of translation and previous apprenticeship with an established translator,
- a sound command of the translator's working languages,
- a full knowledge of the author of the original work, including his style and idiosyncrasies, and
- translating poetry and other sensitive and culturally bound works was to be avoided unless the translators wrote such texts themselves.

Hunayn ibn Ishaq, the great translator of all and the most important figure in MAT, was a physician in addition to being bilingual with Syriac as his first language. Zaydan (2000) reports that recorded history shows that Hunayn ibn Ishaq produced well over 112 translations, predominantly in the medical sciences, at a time when book production technology was very basic and time consuming. The brief biography, given in appendix A of this prolific translator and scholar, only hints at his cultural and historic importance and contributions to intercultural communication into Arabic and later into European languages. Not only was Ibn Ishaq a great translator, he was also a great organizer and manager of translation activity and an important contributor to translation theory.

MAT: A HISTORIOGRAPHICAL ASSESSMENT

MAT did not happen in a cultural vacuum or in isolation from the cultures and ideologies that surrounded Arab/Islamic lands. Armed with their new religion and its linguistic medium, Arabic, the Arabs/Muslims certainly practised what one may call religious and cultural elitism. To strengthen their new state, they needed everything except for religion, poetry and language. Although translators usually tried to follow the original text as closely as possible, they often added bits of information from their own knowledge or deleted bits of information that did not confirm with their belief system: "traces of paganism were eliminated and substituted by references more in accordance with their own beliefs" (Kruk, 1976, 18).

Medieval Arab translators marginalized certain canons, but they did not try to wholly domesticate them, in the sense Venuti (1998) assigns to the concept. Rather, they used intricate adaptive or compensatory strategies in transferring works into Arabic. Were they invisible or subverters? I would argue that the answer lies more in *their culture of translation* and less in *their translation of culture*; a clear cultural (ideological) agenda was the thrust behind and catalyst for their translation practice.

The historiographical importance of medieval Arab translators as intercultural mediators is perhaps better appreciated in the assessment given by others as in the following citation from Burnett (1992, 1050):

> The Arabs of the Middle Ages seem to have had a special flair for mathematics, and the Latin translations in this field provide only a dim reflection of the true splendour of the achievements of men like al-Mu'taman b. Hūd or Omar Khayyam. The translations did, however, introduce into the West calculation with Arabic numerals, algebra, trigonometry and advanced geometry. In medicine, above all, Arabic works became familiar in the Latin forms of Avicenna (this time as author of the *Canon of Medicine*), Rhazes, Mesue, Issac, and Abulcasim.

Medieval European scholars also stated the same. Echoing the views of many of his contemporaries, Hugo of Santalla, for example, wrote: "It befits us to imitate the Arabs especially, for they are as it were our teachers and precursors" (cited in Burnett, 1992: 1051).

While purely practical considerations triggered the movement of MAT, it was ideological (that is cultural in the broadest sense of the term) considerations that pushed it to its zenith but also signalled its demise. Its Omayyad time was witnessed by sporadic, *ad hoc* activities and projects. Its Abbasid time, on the other hand, was more organized and prolific. The great achievements of this historically unique enterprise reflected the collective cultural and civilizational development of the Arab/Islamic nation then and translation was a natural response to and reflection of the demands posed by such development. Also, the intellectual, or rather ideological and philosophical orientation of the Caliphs shaped the trends of and the demands put on translation and translators.

From the start, MAT was not an end in itself. Translated texts were often used to stretch intellectual capabilities. Through appropriation of the scientific and philosophical heritage of others, medieval Arab translators helped to develop a unique Arab/Islamic cultural identity. Translators were educators of their community and popularizers of the scholarship of other cultures. Much appreciated by all sectors of the *Ummah* (nation), their work became the catalyst for native scholarship and the production of essentially Arab/Islamic works, the foundations of an empire that lasted for centuries.

Cultural hegemony was practised. Medieval Arab translators translated little literature because, on the one hand, they were proud of their own and, on the other, because Greek literature contained ideas and myths that were not compatible with their belief system. In this context, Lewis (1994, 75) remarks:

> [T]he literature of an alien and heathen society could offer neither aesthetic appeal nor moral guidance. The history of these remote peoples, without prophets or scriptures, was a mere sequence of events, without aim or meaning. [For the medieval Arab translator], literature meant the poetry and eloquence of his own rich cultural tradition.

One could argue that medieval Arab translators managed more than they monitored. But then, their interest in translation did not spring from a genuine interest in Greek or any other culture: it was prompted by their urgent need to satisfy the necessities of a young nation. Thus, they carried out considerable negation of the strangeness of the foreign works. But in all historical epochs translators' fundamental choices are governed by the interests of patrons, states, publishers, editors, etc.

Culturally, MAT was the tool for an interactive dialogue between the Arab/Muslim nation and other cultures, but most importantly it was seen as the means for state and identity building through the manipulation of Greek and other nations' intellectual heritage. MAT served to establish a culture that was characterized by the following points:

- A large scale and sustained movement of publication of native and translated works.
- An organized, state-sponsored translation movement.
- A wide diffusion of native and translated works.

- Truly competent-cum-expert translators.
- An open 'shopping-list' of source texts that covered all areas of knowledge and scholarship of all cultures of the time.
- Clear policies for translation as a project of national importance and pride.
- Clear language planning that assisted the translation movement.
- Collective efforts and clear strategies in dealing with and solving the problematics of terminology.
- A strategic planning for the choice of texts for translation.
- Generous funding.

This is a far cry from the dire situation of modern Arabic translation to which the complete opposite of the ten points aptly apply.

Translations, according to Simon (1996), become symbolically the very representation of equivalence between different cultures on the basis, I would add, of specific cultures of translation. For MAT, it was a new religion, Islam that encouraged believers to do two things: to spread the new faith and to promote scholarship of their own. Within two centuries, the Arabs/Muslims managed to do both. They carved out a large empire and, at the same time, translated widely from the languages and cultures they came in contact with. Consequently, centres of culture and splendour unrivalled in their time were created in Baghdad in the east and in Cordoba in the west – Muslim Spain. The late André Lefevere (1996, 55) eloquently described something akin to the practice of the medieval Arab translator:

> Translators . . . are not mere passive conduits through which messages pass from one language to another (perhaps unwittingly, but never more forcefully symbolized by the decontextualized, dehistoricized, and degendered 'boxes,' linked by incredibly straight 'arrows' in the early textbooks on translation) but as active negotiators between cultures, whose negotiations may, if not change the face of cultures all on their own, at least heavily contribute to doing so. As much, they are not only worthy of study, but they also provide an incredibly fertile storehouse of materials for the study of cultural relations, acculturation, and multiculturalism.

As a culturally motivated enterprise, MAT managed to strike a balance between the universe of knowledge—as a human activity—and the universe of its master discourse with its own cultural guidelines and discursive norms. It would indeed be beneficial to learn from MAT and the particular culture it helped to build at a time when our contemporary world is in a dire need for human, non-violent, non-stereotypical, and certainly non-isolationist translation practices and projects. Such a need can be met by considering in a contrastive fashion how different cultural traditions view translation and the process and politics of translating. Projects and movements for translating cultures should be viewed and evaluated within the context of their cultures that trigger them in the first place.

Unfortunately, the treatment of translation theory and practice has generally neglected this crucial area. We could learn so much from an informed assessment of the practices of previous translators and translation movements. MAT played a vital historiographical role in the cultural development not only of the Arab/Islamic world, but also of other worlds and cultures: a true mission of translation as intercultural communication.

Appendix

Inb Ishaq, Hunayn (809-73); known as Joannitius in the West. A Nestorian Christian from al-Hira (in modern-day Iraq), nicknamed the 'Prince of Translators,' Ibn Ishaq was among the most gifted and productive translators during the Abbasid period [750-1258]. Bilingual in Arabic and Syriac, he studied medicine . . . went on to learn Greek and then began his career as physician and translator in Baghdad. He headed Bayt al-Hikma . . . where he took charge of all scientific translation work and, with his son Ishaq, his nephew and other students and members of his school, translated into Syriac and Arabic the bulk of Greek medical material known at the time, many of Aristotle's works (including *Categories*, *Physics* and *Magna Moralia*), Plato's *Republic*, works by Hippocrates, various treatises on mathematics and physics, as well as the Septuagint. . . . [H]e enriched Arabic with a very large number of scientific terms. . . . [He] was a conscientious and sophisticated translator who took great pains to verify the accuracy of a source text before proceeding with the translation. He also adopted a sense-for-sense approach which distinguished his work from many crude, literal translations of the time.

Author Index

Subject Index